100
Soups
for $5 or Less

100
Soups
for $5 or Less

Gayle Pierce

GIBBS SMITH
TO ENRICH AND INSPIRE HUMANKIND
Salt Lake City | Charleston | Santa Fe | Santa Barbara

First Edition
10 11 12 13   5 4 3 2

Text © 2009 Gayle Pierce

Published by
Gibbs Smith
P.O. Box 667
Layton, Utah 84041

1-800.835.4993 orders
www.gibbs-smith.com

Cover designed by Natalie Peirce
Printed and bound in Canada
Gibbs Smith books are printed on either recycled, 100% post-
consumer waste, FSC-certified papers or on paper produced from
a 100% certified sustainable forest/controlled wood source.

Library of Congress Cataloging-in-Publication Data

Pierce, Gayle.
100 soups for $5 or less / Gayle Pierce. — 1st ed.
p. cm.
ISBN-13: 978-1-4236-0652-9
ISBN-10: 1-4236-0652-3
1. Soups. 2. Low budget cookery. I. Title. II. Title: One
hundred soups for five dollars or less.
TX757.P543 2009
641.8'13—dc22
2009010203

For Carolyn Thornton, my mom—
the best "pinch of this" cook I know.
And
For Casey Jo Pierce, my daughter—
the inspiration for everything I do.

Contents

Acknowledgments

I would like to extend a heartfelt "Thank You" to the friends and neighbors (past and present) who were willing to try new concoctions and take the time to give me valuable feedback. My love and appreciation to all of you.

Introduction

Now is the time to examine your food budget and develop savvy shopping and cooking skills that will benefit you and your whole family. This book is full of tips and advice on how to save money on food—one of the few areas of spending you can actually control. Besides providing you with budget-saving techniques, this book also offers 100 imaginative recipes made from low-cost ingredients that will please anyone who tries them. Let the saving begin!

Have a Plan Before You Shop

The key to staying within your food budget is to have a plan. In the case of grocery shopping, your plan should include a grocery list. Once you have a list, stick to it! Check out the following suggestions for creating the perfect grocery-shopping list.

1. Do you know what's on sale? Local grocery stores typically send out fliers in the mail or newspaper each week. Take advantage of these fliers and use them to help make your weekly grocery list. Start your list by writing down the store, sale item, and price. After you've put your list together (including ingredients from the recipes you will be making), review it. Is there something you can eliminate? After a few weeks of smart shopping and thrifty cooking, you'll start to see places on your grocery list where you can really cut back.

NOTE: Smart spenders know that the key to the greatest savings depends on purchasing the best sale items. Combined with coupons, the grocery items on sale can be purchased at greatly reduced prices.

2. Look ahead a week or two when making out your shopping list. This means planning out the recipes you intend to make ahead of time as well. In your planning, consider what you already have in your pantry, refrigerator, or freezer that could be used in combination with, or as a substitute for, ingredients in upcoming recipes you want to make. This method will prevent you from buying unnecessary groceries and will also help to use up any leftovers that might be looming in your kitchen.

3. Many ingredients are common in multiple recipes, so consider looking for recipes to make each week that share some of the same ingredients but are different enough to provide delicious variety for your family. Also, think about recipes that would be easy to double and freeze for later use.

4. Where is the best place to shop? Most people go to the supermarket or store that is the closest or most convenient for them. Since you've already made a grocery list of stores and sale items, try to stick to the list and shop at those places instead. However, keep in mind that it isn't worth spending a dollar in gas to save twenty-five cents on a single food item. **NOTE:** Some grocery stores offer price matching for sale items. Just ask the customer service desk if they offer the service and what you will need to do to benefit from it.

5. Clipping coupons really does cut costs. In short, some people are meant to be coupon clippers and some are not. While some find it frustrating and time-consuming to clip coupons for everything, there are those who do it and love it. Just remember to clip coupons for things you normally buy; just because you have a coupon for something doesn't mean you have to buy it. If it's something out of the ordinary, getting it at a reduced price still means you're spending outside of your budget to get it. **NOTE:** Many stores have double-coupon days. This means the store matches the discount on the coupon and you save double the amount!

General Grocery Shopping Tips

Even if you are armed with the best-ever shopping list, it's tough to get in and out of the store as planned without a whole lot of will power. Things such as store layout, time of day, your state of mind, and really powerful marketing techniques are at work to get you to spend more money. For those who are new to food budgeting, this might all seem a bit overwhelming. However, with a few weeks of practice, you'll find that you're planning meals and shopping like a pro. The following tips on shopping in general may help guide you in your quest to save money.

» Try to choose a time when you can go to the store with the fewest distractions, whether that means leaving kids at home or avoiding crowds of other shoppers. Try going early in the morning or late at night. Generally, avoid the after-work rush and anytime after 11:00 a.m. on weekends.

» Go to the grocery store as infrequently as you can. Try going once a week to coincide with the weekly fliers. The easiest way to blow your food budget is to go the store multiple times each week for a few items, because most likely you'll leave the store with more than you intended. If you can make do with what you have at home, you will save money every month.

» Don't shop when you're hungry or thirsty. If this can't be avoided, try drinking water before you go shopping to take the edge off your appetite.

» When walking down the aisles, look low and high for the less expensive brands. Most stores place the brand-name products on eye-level shelves because shoppers tend to grab whatever is in front of them instead of looking for the best bargains.

» Stay focused on the price of the item, not the packaging it comes in. Since bright colors and fancy packaging are attractive, shoppers tend to pick up these items first. House brands are generally less colorful but typically less expensive.

» Remember to stick to your list to avoid impulse buying. When you pick up something that isn't on your list, ask yourself why you want it. Do you really *need* it or do you just *want* it? Too many impulse purchases can ruin your carefully planned food budget.

» It is a huge advantage to know which fruits and vegetables are in season, as they will be part of some great sales. Not only are in-season produce items less expensive, they're fresher. It's also wise to learn which vegetables and fruits are less expensive when fresh, and which ones are less expensive when frozen or canned.

NOTE: Beware of the conveniently packaged produce designed to save you time in preparation. Most of these convenience items cost twice as much.

» Remember to check the weekly fliers for sales on your family's favorite snack foods. Everyone loves snacks, and it's easy to spend a lot on salty and sugary items if they aren't on sale.

» The frozen food section is the home of some of the best grocery bargains, as well as some of the worst. Remember, convenience often comes with a price. On the flip side, there are some frozen foods that cost much less than fresh or canned, and they are often healthier because the vitamin content is preserved when they are flash frozen.

20 Budget-Saving Tips

The following list includes the best budget-saving tips in a nutshell:

1. Use coupons. Though this doesn't really need an explanation, clipping coupons is an excellent way to save. See if the grocer in your area has a double- or triple-coupon day for even more savings.

2. Know your family's likes and dislikes. Stock up on favorites when they are on sale and skip sales of items your family doesn't like.

3. Look for recipes that require a few inexpensive ingredients and avoid those that require you to buy something you'll rarely use again, such as an exotic spice.

4. Experiment with recipes. If you're making a soup that calls for cumin and you have chili powder, use what you have.

5. Substitute less-expensive ingredients for expensive ones. Determine if the recipe absolutely must have that item to make it work. If not, leave it out altogether or use a cheaper alternative. For example, using chicken bouillon cubes instead of chicken broth works in many recipes.

6. Use a lesser amount of an expensive ingredient if you can't find a substitute for it. For example, try cutting the amount by a third. Keep cutting each time you make the recipe to see how it tastes. Once the adjustment is noticeable, you know you've cut too much.

7. Buy store brands. These brands are generally less expensive and usually just as good as name brands—sometimes even better.

8. Think of ways to use everything you already have. Maybe you will create an amazing new soup!

9. Substitute canned fruit for fresh if a recipe calls for a fruit that is not in season or when it won't sacrifice taste.

10. Reduce meat consumption. Try using ½ pound ground beef when a recipe calls for 1 pound and add more rice or vegetables to compensate. Most likely your family won't even notice.

11. Save or bookmark recipes that your family really likes so you know what ingredients to stock in your pantry.

12. Double a soup recipe so you can enjoy it several nights of the week.

13. Always have the ingredients of a tried-and-true "standby" soup in your pantry.

14. Buy in bulk. Though the upfront cost is a little more, you'll be able to get more uses out of bulk item purchases, making the actual costs per serving much less.

15. Freezing is a great way to preserve the quality of foods until you can use them, especially if you're buying in bulk. Store items such as fruits or vegetables in 1-cup portions so they are easy to grab.

16. Invest in basic food storage items. Simple plastic containers with lids, freezer bags, and aluminum foil can keep food fresh and protected until you need it again.

17. Don't order soup at restaurants. You can make a great pot of chowder or stew at home for much less!

18. Don't sacrifice taste for low-cost items. The key is making delicious and nutritious soups that satisfy.

19. Think healthy and implement low-cost yet nutritious foods into your diet.

20. Control portions. We tend to eat portions that far exceed what we actually need. Once you get used to smaller portions, you'll find that you are satisfied on less. Consult nutrition guides for accurate portions and servings, such as MyFoodDiary.com.

The Well-Stocked Budget Pantry and Refrigerator

When planning for recipes, there are a number of items that a well-stocked budget pantry and refrigerator should include. The following list is by no means inclusive, but it does list grocery items that are traditionally considered staples and that are inexpensive, store well, and are versatile enough to appear in many different dishes without being boring. Keep track of what ingredients you use most often, and if you see one of the must-have items on sale, stock up!

Try to keep these items in your pantry or refrigerator:

» Biscuit baking mixes
» Breads
» Canned cream soups
» Canned vegetables
» Cereals
» Cheeses
» Chips and crackers
» Condiments
» Cornmeal
» Cream, condensed milk, and evaporated milk
» Dry beans and canned beans
» Eggs
» Flour
» Frozen fruit and canned fruit
» Frozen mixed vegetables
» Lemon juice
» Margarine, butter, shortening, and cooking oils
» Meats
» Milk
» Pasta
» Peanut butter
» Potatoes
» Rice
» Salt, pepper, and spices
» Sugar (white, brown, and powdered)

Author's Notes

Growing up and watching my mom cook every meal from scratch taught me two practical kitchen lessons that I want to share with you: plan ahead and use what you have on hand. I knew without a doubt that pot roast dinners at our family table would be followed the next day with vegetable beef soup. You can apply these same principles to your meal preparation. If you have broccoli florets left from a weekend snack tray, make Cream of Broccoli Soup (see page 37), which you can pair with a side of smoked ham for tonight. Use the leftover ham for Navy Beans and Ham (see page 46), which can be made ahead of time, giving you an easy nutritious meal tomorrow. Give your dinner leftovers a good look before stacking them in the back of the fridge. Ask yourself how you can reuse or reinvent these items.

As you peruse these recipes, you will notice a common thread weaving through the collection. Each soup contains herbs or spices—natural seasonings that enhance the taste of ordinary ingredients. These distinctive flavorings, like soup itself, intertwine all cultures, without regard to borders.

Emma Ewing, a woman ahead of her time, wrote the first known American pamphlet dedicated to soups, called *Soup and Soup Making*, which was published in Chicago in 1882. Believing that soup was "convenient, economic and healthful," she lauded the qualities that we have come to expect from food in modern life. "Soup" she said, "must not be a weak, sloppy, characterless compound." And holding the same high standards for soup over a hundred years ago that we do now, she added that it "must be skillfully prepared, so as to please the eye and gratify the palate."

Light Soups

Summer Pasta Soup

Parsley is a delightfully easy herb to grow. It is as comfortable providing a lacy backdrop to a colorful patchwork garden as perched on a sunny kitchen windowsill. The subtle, familiar taste of parsley works as a partner in recipes, linking and enhancing neighboring flavors.

4 chicken bouillon cubes
1/4 cup minced onion
1 teaspoon dried parsley
4 cups water
1/2 cup dried gemelli pasta (small twists)
2 cups fresh store-bought broccoli coleslaw

Add bouillon, onion, and parsley to water in a 3-quart saucepan over medium-high heat; bring to a boil. Reduce heat to low and add pasta. Cover, with lid slightly vented, and cook 10 minutes. Stir in coleslaw. Remove from heat, cover tightly with lid, and let stand 5 minutes. Vegetables will retain a firm texture.

Serves 4

Calories per serving 48
Fat per serving <1g

Egg Drop Soup

Unseen by the human eye, the eggshell has thousands of pores over its surface through which it can absorb flavors and odors. The best way to store your eggs in the refrigerator is in their original cartons. With this recipe, it is very important to prepare your egg beforehand so you can work quickly when the broth begins to boil.

1 egg
4 chicken bouillon cubes
1/4 teaspoon sesame seed oil
4 cups water
2 tablespoons dried chives, for garnish

Break the egg into a small bowl and beat with a fork until well blended; set aside. Add bouillon and sesame oil to water in a 3-quart saucepan over high heat; bring to a boil. Give a quick stir to the egg and, using the fork, drizzle egg into the boiling broth. Continue boiling soup for 30 seconds, then remove from heat. Ladle into serving dishes and garnish with chives.

Serves 4

Calories per serving 19
Fat per serving 1g

Ginger Soup with Spinach

Instead of putting the spinach leaves into the soup, place them in a decorative bowl in a central location on the table. Serve the broth steaming hot and allow guests to add their own spinach.

4 chicken bouillon cubes
¹⁄₄ teaspoon ground ginger
¹⁄₂ cup minced onion
4 cups water
2 tightly packed cups torn spinach leaves

Add bouillon, ginger, and onion to the water in a 3-quart saucepan over medium-high heat; bring to a boil. Reduce heat to low; cover and cook 5 minutes. Remove from heat, stir, and ladle into serving dishes. Stir an equal amount of spinach into each serving of hot broth. The spinach will maintain a firm texture.

Serves 4

Calories per serving 19
Fat per serving <1g

Lemon Artichoke Soup with Diced Pimientos

Vibrant in salads and soups, pimientos are most widely recognized as the bright red filler in pitted green olives. Diced sweet pimiento peppers are commonly sold in small jars found in the canned food aisle of your grocery store.

1 (14-ounce) can artichoke hearts, packed in water
4 chicken bouillon cubes
1/4 teaspoon lemon pepper
1/4 teaspoon dried basil leaves
4 cups water
1 (2-ounce) jar diced red pimientos, drained

Drain artichoke hearts. Slice off bottom of artichoke where leaves are attached and discard. Halve each heart, lay out flat, and chop into pieces; set aside.

Add bouillon, lemon pepper, basil, and artichoke hearts to water in a 3-quart saucepan over medium-high heat; bring to a boil. Reduce heat to low; cover, with lid slightly vented, and cook 5 minutes. Remove from heat, ladle into serving dishes, and garnish with pimientos.

Serves 4

Calories per serving 52
Fat per serving <1g

Lite 'n' Easy Cheese Soup

One of the best ways to recycle stale bread is to make your own croutons. Cut four slices of bread into strips, then cube each strip. Melt 1 tablespoon butter, add your favorite herbs, and stir in the bread cubes. Place on a baking sheet and bake at 350°F for 5–7 minutes. Turn the croutons and bake 5–7 minutes more.

1 tablespoon butter or margarine
1/4 cup finely chopped onion
1 1/2 cups water
2 chicken bouillon cubes
1/4 teaspoon cayenne pepper
2 cups milk
1 tablespoon flour
2 cups finely shredded cheddar cheese
1 cup seasoned croutons, lightly crushed

Combine butter and onion over medium heat in a 3-quart saucepan. Sauté onions until tender. Add water, bouillon, and cayenne pepper. Pour milk into a tall glass; add flour and stir rapidly with a fork until smooth. Add milk mixture to the soup and stir occasionally while bringing to a light boil. Add cheese and stir continuously until melted. Ladle soup into serving dishes and sprinkle each serving with croutons.

Serves 4

Calories per serving 205
Fat per serving 12g

Mushroom Soup with Fresh Spinach

Adding cilantro at the end of the cooking process enables it to maintain more of its distinctive citrus taste. This multi-tasking herb is also the source of coriander seeds. Leftover mushroom stems can be sautéed in butter and served over meat at your next meal.

1/2 pound mushrooms, sliced
6 chicken bouillon cubes
1/2 cup chopped onion
1/2 cup chopped red bell pepper
6 cups water
1 teaspoon dried cilantro leaves
2 heavily packed cups torn spinach leaves

Remove and reserve mushroom stems for another use. Thinly slice the mushroom tops; set aside. Add bouillon, onion, and bell pepper to water in a 3-quart saucepan over medium-high heat. Bring to a light boil, then reduce heat to low. Cover and cook 5 minutes. Add sliced mushrooms and cilantro to broth. Cover with lid and continue to cook over low heat an additional 5 minutes. Remove from heat. Drop in spinach, cover for 1 minute, stir, and then serve.

Serves 6

Calories per serving 26
Fat per serving <1g

Itsy Bitsy Noodle Soup

One of the fine herbs of French cuisine, chervil has a subtle, tender flavor that features hints of anise and parsley. The dainty chervil plant, with its fernlike structure, is a complement to marjoram in this recipe.

2 chicken bouillon cubes
$1/2$ cup chopped green onions, white and green stems
$2/3$ cup frozen peas
2 cups fine (very thin) egg noodles
$1/8$ teaspoon salt
$1/4$ teaspoon dried marjoram
$1/8$ teaspoon dried chervil
5 cups water
1 medium tomato

Add bouillon, green onions, peas, noodles, salt, marjoram, and chervil to water in a 3-quart saucepan over medium-high; bring to a light boil. Reduce heat to low; cover with lid and cook 5 minutes. Peel skin from tomato and chop into bite-size pieces. Add tomato to soup; cover with lid and cook an additional 5 minutes. Remove from heat, stir, and serve.

Serves 6

Calories per serving 88
Fat per serving 1g

Rainbow Sweet Pepper Soup

Sealed plastic sleeves of tri-color sweet bell peppers can be found in most produce departments. They are sometimes labeled "stop light peppers" due to the green, yellow, and red mix. While it is more economical to buy peppers in this manner, it is important to visually inspect the peppers as well as move your fingers softly around the sleeve to ensure all peppers are firm, which indicates freshness.

1 sleeve of 3 sweet bell peppers (tri-color)
3 chicken bouillon cubes
$1/4$ cup minced onion
$1/2$ teaspoon dried marjoram
3 cups water

Wash peppers and slice into strips. Cut each strip into $1/2$-inch pieces; set aside until needed. Add bouillon, onion, and marjoram to water in a 3-quart saucepan over medium high heat; bring to a boil. Reduce heat to low. Cover, with lid slightly vented, and cook 5 minutes to let flavors mingle. Remove from heat. Add peppers to the broth. Cover with lid and let stand 5 minutes. Ladle into serving dishes. Peppers will retain a firm texture.

Serves 4

Calories per serving 34
Fat per serving <1g

Tomato Broth with Corn

This colorful soup with an uncomplicated structure was created from a childhood memory of a well-known Southern side dish: corn and tomatoes.

3 chicken bouillon cubes
1 (8-ounce) can tomato sauce
$1/2$ teaspoon dried oregano
$1/2$ teaspoon dried chives
$1/8$ teaspoon salt
Dash of black pepper
3 cups water
1 cup frozen corn
1 cup shredded zucchini

Add bouillon, tomato sauce, oregano, chives, salt, and pepper to water in a 3-quart saucepan over medium-high heat. Stir in the corn and zucchini; bring to a boil. Reduce heat to low. Cover, with lid slightly vented, and cook 5 minutes. Remove from heat.

Serves 4

Calories per serving 38
Fat per serving <1g

Beef Broth with Shredded Cabbage

Lending its yellow hue to the broth, earthy turmeric is the perfect companion for this cabbage-based soup. Use care when working with turmeric, as it is a powerful dye. Wipe all spills with a paper towel.

4 beef bouillon cubes
1/4 cup chopped onion
1/8 teaspoon turmeric
2 cups shredded cabbage
4 cups water
1/4 cup minced green bell pepper

Add bouillon, onion, turmeric, and cabbage to water in a 3-quart saucepan over medium-high heat. Bring to a low boil, then remove from heat. Cover tightly with lid and let stand 5 minutes. Cabbage will retain a firm texture. Ladle into serving dishes and sprinkle bell pepper into each bowl.

Serves 4

Calories per serving 15
Fat per serving <1g

Cream Soups

Cream of Asparagus

Heavy cream, while not on the low-calorie menu, is a food experience rich in flavor and texture. The difference in light and heavy cream is the fat content. One is not a substitute for the other. If you can't find heavy cream, use ³/₄ cup milk mixed with ¹/₄ cup butter (not margarine) for each 1 cup of heavy cream.

1 (15-ounce) can asparagus spears, drained
5 cups water
5 chicken bouillon cubes
1 cup diced potatoes
¹/₄ cup diced onion
¹/₄ teaspoon ground white pepper
¹/₈ teaspoon ground nutmeg
³/₄ cup heavy cream

Cut off and reserve the feathered tips from asparagus spears; set aside. Cut the spears into 1-inch pieces and place in a 3-quart saucepan over medium-high heat. Add water, bouillon, potatoes, onion, white pepper, and nutmeg; bring to a boil. Reduce heat to low. Cover, with lid slightly vented, and cook 20 minutes. Pour contents of saucepan into a blender and purée. (This may need to be done in batches.) Return soup to saucepan over medium-high heat. Stir in heavy cream and reserved asparagus tips. Bring to a boil, stirring constantly. Remove from heat and ladle into serving dishes.

Serves 6

Calories per serving 142
Fat per serving 11g

Creamy Cauliflower

White pepper comes from the same vine, *Piper nigrum,* as black pepper. Unlike black pepper, where the berries are picked while they are still green and then left to ferment and dry in the sun, the berries for white pepper are left alone until they are fully ripe. The outer layer of skin on the small berry is removed, revealing the grayish-white inner kernel, which is then used whole or ground.

3 cups water
3 chicken bouillon cubes
3 cups cauliflower florets
$1/2$ cup chopped onion
2 tablespoons butter or margarine
$1/2$ teaspoon salt
$1/4$ teaspoon white pepper
$1/8$ teaspoon dill weed, fresh or dried
$1 1/2$ tablespoons flour
1 cup milk
1 cup grated cheddar cheese for garnish

Combine water and bouillon in a 3-quart saucepan over medium-high heat. Add cauliflower, onion, butter, salt, white pepper, and dill weed; bring to a boil. Reduce heat to medium. Cover, with lid slightly vented, and cook 10 minutes. Use a tall glass and stir flour into milk with a fork until smooth. Pour milk mixture into soup, removing any flour lumps (they will float to the top). Cook 5 minutes more, breaking up any large pieces of cauliflower as you stir. Remove from heat, ladle into serving dishes, and garnish with cheese.

Serves 4

Calories per serving 231
Fat per serving 15g

Crushed Corn Chowder

The word "chowder" encompasses a wide range of ingredients based largely on where you call home. Seafood chowder is common fare on the coastal areas whereas vegetable chowders are more familiar inland. Regardless of the primary ingredients, most chowder recipes generally contain milk or cream and are thickened with flour.

1 (1-pound) bag frozen corn
2 cups water
$^1/_2$ cup chopped onion
1 teaspoon salt
$^1/_4$ teaspoon black pepper
$^1/_4$ teaspoon chili powder
1 tablespoon butter or margarine
2 $^1/_2$ tablespoons flour
1 $^1/_2$ cups milk
Dill weed for garnish

Put frozen corn into a blender and run on crush cycle until half of the kernels are powder. Place corn in a 3-quart saucepan over medium-high heat. Add the water, onion, salt, pepper, chili powder, and butter. Bring to a boil, then reduce heat to low. In a tall glass, rapidly stir flour into milk with a fork. Add milk mixture to soup, removing any flour lumps (they will float to the top). Cover with lid and cook over low heat for 10 minutes, stirring occasionally. Ladle soup into serving dishes and sprinkle lightly with dill weed.

Serves 6

Calories per serving 140
Fat per serving 4g

Leek Soup with Thyme

Black pepper is often called the "master spice" because it can be stored for many years without losing its flavor or aroma. Its kinship with white pepper is put aside when taste is compared. Unlike its woodsy tasting sister berry, forceful black pepper registers a notoriously hot bite if used in excess.

2 large leeks
4 chicken bouillon cubes
2 1/2 cups diced potatoes
4 cups water
1 small clove garlic, pressed
1/4 teaspoon ground thyme
1/4 teaspoon salt
1/8 teaspoon black pepper
1/2 cup heavy cream
Dill weed for garnish, fresh or dried

    Remove and discard the tough green outer leek leaves. Clean leeks thoroughly, running water between the leaves. Slice the white and light green part of the leek into 1/2-inch rounds; set aside. Add bouillon, leek rounds, and potatoes to water in a 3-quart saucepan. Stir in garlic, thyme, salt, and pepper; bring to a boil. Reduce heat to low; cover with lid and cook 15 minutes. Pour soup into a blender and purée. Add cream and blend until evenly distributed. Ladle into serving dishes and garnish with dill weed.

Serves 6

Calories per serving 165
Fat per serving 7g

Sweet Southern Onion Soup

To purée a soup is to break it down to a thick liquid, most commonly using a blender. With the exception of fruit soups, ingredients are cooked prior to this process.

4 chicken bouillon cubes
4 cups sliced sweet onions
3 cups sliced potato
4 cups water
1 tablespoon dried chives
¹/₂ teaspoon salt
¹/₄ teaspoon black pepper
¹/₂ cup light cream
¹/₂ cup diced red bell pepper

Add bouillon, onions, and potatoes to water in a 3-quart saucepan over medium-high heat. Stir in chives, salt, and pepper. Push the potatoes down into the broth with a spoon. Bring to a boil, then reduce heat to medium. Cover, with lid slightly vented, and cook 20 minutes. Ladle soup into a blender and purée. (This may need to be done in batches.) Pour puréed soup back into saucepan over medium heat. Stir in the light cream. Leave over heat for 5 minutes, stirring continuously. Remove from heat and ladle into serving dishes. Sprinkle each serving with bell pepper.

Serves 6

Calories per serving 182
Fat per serving 4g

Asian Potato Soup with Kale

A non-heading cabbage, lace-edged kale is commonly used to add interest to soup. When cooking with kale, use the fresh leaves within a few days of purchase or they will develop a bitter taste.

4 chicken bouillon cubes
1 cup chopped onion
1 large clove garlic, thinly sliced
4 cups sliced potato
4 cups water
$1/4$ teaspoon sesame seed oil
2 tablespoons light soy sauce
$1/8$ teaspoon ground ginger
$1/2$ teaspoon salt
$1/8$ teaspoon black pepper
4 cups heavily packed torn kale

Add bouillon, onion, garlic, and potatoes to water in a 3-quart saucepan. Stir in sesame seed oil, soy sauce, ginger, salt, and pepper; bring to a boil. Reduce heat to low and cook, with lid slightly vented, for 10 minutes. Pour soup into a blender and purée until smooth. Return to saucepan over low heat. Stir kale into soup. Cover and cook an additional 10 minutes. Remove from heat. Stir and serve.

Serves 4

Calories per serving 288
Fat per serving 14g

Cream Soups

Baked Potato Soup

The slender and hollow leaves of the chive have the taste of a sweet mild onion. This dark green herb complements almost every flavor. The chive is one of the few herbs that is equally appealing as an ingredient or as a garnish.

3 chicken bouillon cubes
5 cups sliced potatoes
$^1/_2$ teaspoon salt
$^1/_8$ teaspoon black pepper
1 teaspoon chives
3 cups water
1 cup heavy cream
4 strips bacon, cooked crisp and crumbled
$^1/_3$ cup chopped green onions (green part only)
$^1/_2$ cup grated cheddar cheese

Add bouillon, potatoes, salt, pepper, and chives to water in a 3-quart saucepan over medium-high heat. Bring to a boil, then reduce heat to low. Cover, with lid slightly vented, and cook 15 minutes. Pour soup into a blender and purée. Return soup to saucepan over low heat. Pour cream into soup and cook 5 minutes more, stirring occasionally. Ladle into serving bowls. Sprinkle with bacon, green onion, and cheese as garnish.

Serves 4

Calories per serving 564
Fat per serving 38g

Cream of Broccoli

The bright red lacy covering of the nutmeg shell demands as much attention as the brown nutmeg seed itself. This encasement, which shares a similar yet more intense flavor than nutmeg, is known as mace. As mace ages and dries, it loses its brilliant color but gains its familiar scent.

1 (12-ounce) package frozen broccoli pieces
6 chicken bouillon cubes
1/2 cup chopped onion
1/4 teaspoon celery seed
1/8 teaspoon ground mace
2 cups water
1 1/2 cups light cream

Add broccoli, bouillon, onion, celery seed, and mace to water in a 3-quart saucepan over medium-high heat. Bring to a boil, then reduce heat to low. Remove 4 broccoli florets, finely chop the seed heads for garnish and return any stems to the soup. Cover, with lid slightly vented, and cook 5 minutes. Pour soup into a blender and purée until smooth. Return soup to saucepan over low heat. Stir in light cream. Cover with lid and cook 5 minutes more. Garnish with chopped broccoli florets.

Serves 4

Calories per serving 207
Fat per serving 17g

Creamy Sweet Potato Soup

Unlike holiday sweet potatoes coated in cinnamon and brown sugar, this coral-colored vegetable shows its versatility by going to the other end of the spectrum where it is combined with hot red peppers in a beautiful and taste-pleasing soup.

1 $1/2$ pounds sweet potatoes, peeled and sliced
2 chicken bouillon cubes
$1/4$ teaspoon salt
$1/2$ teaspoon ground cumin
$1/4$ teaspoon dried crushed red pepper
2 cups water
1 cup light cream
$1/8$ teaspoon paprika

Add potatoes, bouillon, salt, cumin, and crushed red peppers to water in a 3-quart saucepan over medium-high heat; bring to a boil. Reduce heat to low. Cover, with lid slightly vented, and cook 10 minutes. Pour soup into a blender and purée. Pour soup back into saucepan over low heat. Stir in cream and cook 5 minutes more, stirring frequently. Ladle into serving dishes. Garnish each serving with a sprinkle of paprika.

Serves 4

Calories per serving 271
Fat per serving 11g

Cream of Celery

Pale green celery, with its long ribbed stalks and leafy green top, is a staple ingredient in soups and stews. Celery earned this honor due not only to its unique flavor but also to its affordability.

4 chicken bouillon cubes
1 cup chopped onion
1 clove garlic, thinly sliced
2 cups water
4 cups chopped celery pieces
$1/4$ teaspoon salt
$1/8$ teaspoon black pepper
$1/2$ teaspoon dried oregano
$1/2$ cup heavy cream

Add bouillon, onion, and garlic to water in a 3-quart saucepan over medium-high heat. Add celery to the soup. (Reserve any inner celery leaves for garnish.) Stir salt, pepper, and oregano into soup. Bring to a boil, then reduce heat to low. Cover, with lid slightly vented, and cook 15 minutes. Pour soup into a blender and purée until smooth. Return soup to saucepan over low heat. Stir in cream and cook 5 minutes more, stirring occasionally. Ladle into serving dishes and garnish with celery leaves.

Serves 4

Calories per serving 138
Fat per serving 11g

Bean Soups

Country Simmer

Colorful cayenne pepper, whose pods come in shades of red, orange, or yellow, can cause a volcanic experience if a cook becomes too heavy handed. The eruption of heat lets you know that cayenne, whose name comes from the Greek word meaning "to bite," lives up to its moniker.

2 cups dried pinto beans
12 cups water
1 (28-ounce) can peeled and diced tomatoes, with juice
²/₃ cup frozen corn
1 (9-ounce) package frozen peas and pearl onion mix
2 beef bouillon cubes
¹/₄ teaspoon salt
¹/₈ teaspoon black pepper
¹/₈ teaspoon ground cayenne pepper

Sort and rinse beans. Use a 5-quart pot and combine beans and water over high heat. Bring to a rolling boil. Allow to boil 3–4 minutes, then reduce heat to medium. Cook, covered with lid slightly vented, for 2 hours, stirring occasionally. Add ½ cup more hot water while cooking if needed. Add tomatoes with juice, corn, peas and onion mix, bouillon, salt, pepper, and cayenne pepper. Cook, uncovered, 20 minutes more, stirring occasionally.

Serves 6

Calories per serving 142
Fat per serving <1g

Farm-Style Lentil Soup

The thick, leathery bay leaf is an herb that comes from a tree instead of a plant. Used whole for culinary purposes, the bay leaf has the ability to harmonize flavors. Both fresh and dried bay leaves have sharp edges that do not soften when cooked and should not be eaten. Always remove bay leaves from soups and stews before serving.

1 cup dried lentils
4 cups water
$1/2$ cup chopped onion
$1/2$ cup chopped celery
$1/2$ cup carrot slices
2 chicken bouillon cubes
3 slices bacon, cooked crisp
1 ($14 1/2$-ounce) can diced tomatoes, drained
$1/4$ teaspoon salt
Dash of black pepper
1 whole bay leaf (do not crumble)

Sort and rinse lentils. Add lentils to water in a 3-quart saucepan over medium-high heat and bring to a rolling boil. Let boil 5 minutes. Remove from heat; cover and let stand 30 minutes. Place lentils over medium-high heat. Add onion, celery, carrots, and bouillon. Break bacon into 1-inch pieces and add to soup. Stir in tomatoes, salt, pepper, and bay leaf. Bring soup to a boil, then reduce heat to medium low. Cover with lid and simmer 40 minutes. Remove bay leaf before serving.

Serves 4

Calories per serving 320
Fat per serving 9g

Great Northern Bean Soup

It is always important to sort dried beans and peas. Small stones, which are not teeth friendly, sometimes make their way into the bags through the manufacturing process. If you prefer, navy beans would be a suitable substitution for great Northern beans in this soup.

1 (1-pound) package dried great Northern beans
2 beef bouillon cubes
10 cups water
1 cup chopped onion
1/2 cup chopped celery
1 large clove garlic, minced
1 teaspoon salt
1/4 teaspoon black pepper
2 whole bay leaves (do not crumble)
1/2 cup diced red bell pepper

Sort and rinse beans. Add beans and bouillon to water in a 5-quart pot over high heat. Bring to a boil and let boil 5 minutes. Remove from heat and let stand 1 hour. Return beans to medium heat. Add onion, celery, garlic, salt, pepper, and bay leaves to beans. Cover, with lid slightly vented, and cook 1 hour. Reduce heat to low and remove 2 cups of beans, with no liquid. Mash well and return to soup. Cover, with lid slightly vented, and cook 20 minutes. Add bell pepper and cook 5 minutes more. Remove bay leaves before serving.

Serves 6

Calories per serving 104
Fat per serving <1g

Lentil Soup with Apricots

Apricots are one of the best natural sources of vitamin A and display flavors ranging from sweet to tart with numerous varieties. Fresh apricots are best served in a heavy syrup while dried apricots have versatility as well as longevity.

$1/2$ **pound boneless pork roast**
9 cups water, divided
2 beef bouillon cubes
$1/2$ **cup chopped onion**
$1 1/2$ **cups dried lentils**
$1/4$ **teaspoon salt**
$1/2$ **teaspoon basil**
10 dried apricots

Cut pork roast into quarters for faster cooking. Add pork roast to 5 cups water in a 3-quart saucepan over high heat. Bring to a boil, then reduce heat to low. Cover and cook 20 minutes, or until fully cooked. Remove roast, discard water, and rinse pan. Trim any fat from pork and chop into bite-size pieces; set aside.

Pour 4 cups fresh water into saucepan over medium-high heat. Add pork, bouillon, onion, lentils, salt, and basil. Chop each dried apricot into 9 pieces, and then add to soup. Bring to a boil, then reduce heat to low. Cover, with lid slightly vented, and cook 25 minutes.

Serves 6

Calories per serving 285
Fat per serving 4g

Navy Beans and Ham

A long-standing favorite in many households, navy bean soup can be stored in the refrigerator with an open-ladle policy for up to three days after cooking (or until it runs out, which usually comes first). Add additional water when reheating if needed.

1 ($^1/_2$-pound) bag dried navy beans
6 cups water, divided
$^1/_2$ pound boneless smoked ham, cubed
$^1/_2$ cup chopped onion
1 whole bay leaf (do not crumble)
$^1/_4$ teaspoon salt
$^1/_8$ teaspoon black pepper

    Sort and rinse beans. Bring 4 cups water to a boil in a 3-quart saucepan over medium-high heat. Add navy beans and let boil vigorously for 15 minutes. Reduce heat to medium low; cover and cook 45 minutes more. Add an additional ½ cup water if needed. Add 2 cups fresh water, ham, onion, bay leaf, salt, and pepper. Cover with lid and cook 60 minutes more. Remove bay leaf. Stir and serve.

Serves 4

Calories per serving 189
Fat per serving 5g

Black Bean Soup

Soaking black beans, or turtle beans, as they are also known, softens their hulls and reduces cooking time. Black beans are actually deep purple, a color that is maintained even when cooked. Featuring a small white eye called a "keel" as well as a pleasant earthy taste, the nutritious black bean is a familiar ingredient in soups.

8 ounces dried black beans
5 cups water, plus more for soaking
1/2 pound boneless smoked ham, cubed
1/2 cup chopped onion
1 small clove garlic, pressed
1/4 teaspoon salt
1/8 teaspoon black pepper
1 large whole bay leaf (do not crumble)
1 cup grated mild cheddar cheese

Sort and rinse beans. Place beans in a 3-quart saucepan and cover entirely with water. Cover with lid and refrigerate overnight. The next day, drain water from beans and rinse. Add 5 cups water to beans and place over high heat. Add ham, onion, and garlic. Stir in salt, pepper, and bay leaf. Bring to a rapid boil, then reduce heat to medium low. Cover with lid and cook 2 hours, stirring occasionally. Remove bay leaf from soup. Ladle into serving dishes and garnish with cheese.

Serves 4

Calories per serving 418
Fat per serving 15g

Garbanzo Simmer

Officially known as chickpeas but more commonly called garbanzo beans, this member of the legume family is a good source of protein. The highest quality chickpea in the world is grown in the rich volcanic soil that sits in the rain shadow of the Cascade Mountains in the Pacific Northwest.

4 chicken bouillon cubes
2 (15-ounce) cans prepared garbanzo beans, drained
1/2 cup chopped onion
1 cup grated carrot
1/2 pound boneless ham, cubed
8 cups water
1/8 teaspoon black pepper
1/2 teaspoon cilantro leaves
1/4 cup minced green bell pepper

Add bouillon, garbanzo beans, onion, carrot, and ham to water in a 5-quart pot over medium-high heat. Stir in pepper. Bring to a boil, then reduce heat to low. Cover, with lid slightly vented, and simmer 50 minutes. Add cilantro and cook an additional 10 minutes. Ladle soup into serving dishes and garnish with bell pepper.

Serves 6

Calories per serving 602
Fat per serving 12g

Burly Bean Porridge

Enveloped in a papery wrap, garlic is a compound bulb composed of up to fifteen cloves. This vivacious herb with an onion taste is well suited to all foods—with the exception of sweets.

1/2 **pound dried red kidney beans**
3 **extra large vegetable bouillon cubes (or granules to make 6 cups broth)**
1 **small clove garlic, pressed**
6 **cups water**
1/4 **teaspoon salt**
2 **whole bay leaves (do not crumble)**
1/2 **cup quick-cook rice**

Sort and rinse beans. Add beans, bouillon, and garlic to water in a 3-quart saucepan over medium-high heat. Stir in salt and bay leaves. Bring to a boil and boil 2–3 minutes. Reduce heat to low. Cover, with lid slightly vented, and cook 2 hours. Add rice to beans. Cover with lid and continue to cook over low heat for 10 minutes more. Add additional water if needed. Remove from heat and let stand, covered, 10 minutes. Remove bay leaves before serving.

Serves 4

Calories per serving 163
Fat per serving <1g

Louisiana Bean Soup

The small slender tarragon plant with its anise-like flavor is a friend to multiple meat and vegetable dishes. However, it must be handled carefully when cooking. Its strength can easily dominate other ingredients.

1 (14 1/2-ounce) can diced tomatoes, with juice
1 (15 1/2-ounce) can kidney beans, drained
1 (15 1/2-ounce) can pinto beans, drained
1 (16-ounce) can navy beans, drained
2 cups water
1/4 pound smoked sausage
1/2 cup chopped onion
1 clove garlic, thinly sliced
1/2 teaspoon salt
1/2 teaspoon dried crushed red pepper
1/4 teaspoon dried tarragon

Add tomatoes with juice and beans to water in a 3-quart saucepan over medium-high heat. Cut a thin line lengthwise down the middle of the smoked sausage. Remove the casing and slice the sausage into 1/4-inch rounds; add to soup. Stir in onion, garlic, salt, red peppers, and tarragon. Bring to a boil, then reduce heat to low. Cover, with lid slightly vented, and cook 30 minutes, stirring occasionally.

Serves 6

Calories per serving 257
Fat per serving 3g

Baby Butter Bean

With a taste reminiscent of spice and citrus combined, the tuberous rhizome of the ginger plant is at home in meat, vegetable, and dessert recipes.

8 ounces dried baby butter beans
9 cups water, divided
1 extra large vegetable bouillon cube (or enough
    granules for 2 cups broth)
$1/2$ cup finely chopped onion
1 large clove garlic, thinly sliced
$1/4$ teaspoon salt
$1/2$ teaspoon dried crushed red pepper
$1/8$ teaspoon ground ginger

Sort and rinse beans. Add beans to 4 cups water in a 3-quart saucepan over high heat. Bring to a boil and boil 2 minutes. Remove from heat. Cover with lid and let beans stand 1 hour. Drain the soaking water from beans. Add 5 cups fresh water to beans and place over medium-high heat. Add bouillon, onion, garlic, salt, red peppers, and ginger. Bring to a boil, then reduce heat to low. Cover, with lid slightly vented, and cook 2 hours. Check beans. Cook another 15 minutes if needed. Stir and serve.

Serves 4

Calories per serving 91
Fat per serving <1g

Beef Soups

Meatball Stew

The meatballs in this soup can be made a day ahead and stored in an airtight container in the refrigerator. They can also be made a month ahead and frozen until needed. Thaw completely before using.

1 egg
1/2 pound ground chuck
4 beef bouillon cubes
1 (8-ounce) can tomato sauce
1 cup diced carrots
1 1/2 cups grated potato
2/3 cup frozen peas
1/2 cup chopped onion
4 cups water
1/4 teaspoon salt
1/8 teaspoon black pepper
1/2 teaspoon dried oregano

Combine egg and ground chuck in a bowl; mix well. Shape the meat into 18 meatballs. Cook meatballs in a skillet, turning frequently, over medium heat until well done. Remove from pan and refrigerate until needed.

Add bouillon, tomato sauce, carrots, potato, peas, and onion to water in a large saucepan over medium heat. Stir in salt, pepper, and oregano. Add the fully cooked meatballs. Bring to a boil. Reduce heat to low. Cover with lid and cook 15 minutes, stirring occasionally. Remove from heat and ladle into serving dishes, putting three meatballs in each bowl.

Serves 6

Calories per serving 129
Fat per serving 3g

Hanging by a Thread

Thin, transparent threads made from mung beans do not exhibit a notable flavor of their own, instead acquiring the taste of fellow ingredients. Bean threads usually come in packages of four 1-ounce bundles. They are found in the Asian section of the grocery store.

¹/₂ pound ground chuck
1 tablespoon soy sauce
¹/₂ cup chopped green onions, white and green stems
¹/₂ teaspoon minced fresh ginger
8 cups water, divided
2 ounces bean threads (transparent noodles)
4 chicken bouillon cubes
2 packed cups torn kale leaves

  Place the ground chuck in a small bowl. Add soy sauce, green onions, and ginger; stir until all ingredients are evenly distributed. Shape into 1-inch balls (about 15 meatballs). Cook the meatballs in a skillet, place on paper towels to drain, and refrigerate until needed.
  Bring 4 cups water to a boil in a 3-quart saucepan over high heat. Remove from heat. Lay bean threads in the hot water, completely submerging. Cover with lid and let stand 10 minutes. Drain water and move the threads to a plate. Draw a knife through the threads five or six times to cut; set aside. Add bouillon and the fully cooked meatballs to the remaining 4 cups water in the saucepan over high heat. Bring to a boil. Reduce heat to medium. Add kale to soup. Stir in bean threads. Cover with lid and cook an additional 5 minutes. Stir and serve.

Serves 4

Calories per serving 190
Fat per serving 3g

Beef and Barley

If using whole grain barley in the place of "quick-cook" or "pearl" barley (hulled or hull-less), watch that your cooking time is at least 50–55 minutes. Whole grain barley also absorbs less liquid, so it may be necessary to remove at least a cup of the broth before serving.

$^3/_4$ **pound boneless stew beef**
5 cups water
2 beef bouillon cubes
$^1/_2$ **cup quick-cook or pearl barley**
$^1/_2$ **cup carrot slices**
1 (14$^1/_2$-ounce) can diced tomatoes, drained
$^1/_4$ **cup chopped onion**
$^1/_4$ **teaspoon salt**
$^1/_8$ **teaspoon black pepper**
Dash of ground cayenne pepper
1 whole bay leaf (do not crumble)

Cut stew beef into bite-size pieces, removing all fat. Sear all sides of beef in a 3-quart saucepan over high heat. Pour water over beef. Add bouillon, barley, and carrots to pan. Stir in tomatoes, onion, salt, pepper, cayenne pepper, and bay leaf. Bring to a boil. Reduce heat to medium low. Cover with lid and cook 20 minutes, stirring occasionally. Remove bay leaf before serving.

Serves 4

Calories per serving 272
Fat per serving 7g

Stuffed Pepper Soup

The taste of this soup hints of a favorite lunch special served at diner counters in small towns across the country—stuffed green peppers. Cook the ground beef and onions ahead of time and freeze in an airtight container. Having that step complete will enable you to prepare this soup in less than 15 minutes.

¹/₂ pound ground beef
¹/₂ cup chopped onion
3 cups water
1 (15-ounce) can tomato sauce
1 cup chopped green bell pepper
4 beef bouillon cubes
¹/₂ teaspoon dried oregano
1 cup quick-cook rice

Cook ground beef and onion in a skillet over medium heat, stirring frequently to break up large pieces of meat. Drain fat from meat. Pour water into a 3-quart saucepan over medium-high heat. Add meat and onions, tomato sauce, bell pepper, bouillon, and oregano. Bring to a boil. Add rice. Remove from heat, cover tightly with a lid, and let stand 5 minutes.

Serves 6

Calories per serving 228
Fat per serving 5g

Armchair Quarterback Chili

This is a great recipe to make ahead of time and freeze. Ladle the chili into quart-size freezer bags. Check the seals, letting out trapped air. Lay the bags flat on a cooking tray with edges (in case a bag opens); freeze. After the bags are frozen, remove the tray and stack the flat bags. This is a real space saver!

1/2 pound ground chuck
1/2 cup chopped onion (1 small onion)
1 clove garlic, minced
2 cups water
1 (15-ounce) can tomato sauce
1 (15 1/2-ounce) can light red kidney beans, drained
1 (15 1/2-ounce) can hot chili beans in chili gravy
1 1/2 cups chopped celery
1/2 cup diced green bell pepper
1 tablespoon Worcestershire sauce
1/4 teaspoon salt
1/8 teaspoon ground cumin
1/8 teaspoon ground cayenne pepper

Cook ground chuck, onion, and garlic in a 3-quart saucepan over medium heat until well done, stirring frequently to break up large pieces of meat. Drain any grease from meat. Stir water into meat, continuing to cook over medium heat. Add tomato sauce, kidney beans, chili beans with gravy, celery, bell pepper, and Worcestershire sauce. Stir in salt, cumin, and cayenne pepper. Bring to a light boil. Reduce heat to low. Cover with lid and cook 20 minutes, stirring occasionally. Remove from heat, stir, and serve.

Serves 6

Calories per serving 234
Fat per serving 6g

Vegetable Broth with Herbed Meatballs

The pleasingly bitter taste of sage, which has hints of citrus and camphor, is most famous for its use in stuffing. In this soup, sage joins other ingredients in an appetizing arrangement.

1 pound lean ground beef
1 teaspoon dried chives
$^1/_2$ teaspoon ground sage
1 egg
1$^1/_2$ cups dried green split peas
2 extra large vegetable bouillon cubes (or enough granules for 4 cups broth)
1 cup grated carrot
8 cups water

Place ground beef in a mixing bowl. Add chives, sage, and egg. Mix until the ingredients are evenly distributed. Shape the mix into 1-inch balls (about 30 meatballs). Cook the meatballs thoroughly in a skillet over medium heat, browning the outside. Place on a paper towels to drain; refrigerate.

Sort and rinse split peas. Add the peas, bouillon, and carrot to water in a 5-quart saucepan over high heat. Bring to a rolling boil. Reduce heat to medium. Cover, with lid slightly vented, and cook 60 minutes, stirring occasionally.

Add fully cooked meatballs to the soup. Reduce heat to low. Cover with lid and cook 10 minutes more. Remove from heat.

Serves 6

Calories per serving 318
Fat per serving 6g

Montana Beef with Rice

The sweet taste of rosemary, with a hint of pine and a slight suggestion of ginger, is suitable for meat as well as vegetable dishes. The hearty personality of this herb makes it a natural enhancement for soups and stews.

$1/_2$ **pound stew beef, cubed into bite-size pieces**
4 cups water
1 cup carrot slices
1 cup frozen corn
1 (8-ounce) can tomato sauce
4 beef bouillon cubes
$1/_2$ **cup chopped onion**
1 clove garlic, thinly sliced
$1/_8$ **teaspoon salt**
Dash of black pepper
$1/_4$ **teaspoon dried rosemary**
1 cup quick-cook rice

Sear beef until browned on all sides in a 3-quart saucepan over high heat. Pour water over beef. Add all remaining ingredients except rice. Bring to a rolling boil, then reduce heat to low. Cover, with lid slightly vented, and cook 15 minutes. Add rice; remove from heat and cover tightly with lid. Let stand 5 minutes.

Serves 4

Calories per serving 235
Fat per serving 5g

Beef Soups

Beef and Broccoli Soup

The roots of a freshwater aquatic plant, water chestnuts are gaining ground as an ingredient with flexibility. The firm and crunchy texture of this vegetable will hold its posture when cooked in soup.

$1/2$ pound boneless stew beef
4 beef bouillon cubes
1 tablespoon soy sauce
$1/8$ teaspoon ground ginger
1 (8-ounce) can sliced water chestnuts
1 (6-ounce) package frozen broccoli florets
4 cups water

Using a sharp knife, remove fat from beef and julienne. Sear meat strips on all sides in a skillet over high heat.

Add cooked beef, bouillon, soy sauce, ginger, water chestnuts, and broccoli to water in a 3-quart saucepan over medium-high heat. (If broccoli florets are large, let cook 1 minute to thaw, then remove from pan and separate.) Bring soup to a boil. Reduce heat to low. Cover, with lid slightly vented, and cook 5 minutes. Remove from heat. Vegetables will be firm.

Serves 4

Calories per serving 147
Fat per serving 4g

Beef and Noodle Soup

Searing is a process that requires your undivided attention. Always use dry meat and a very hot pan over high heat. Searing converts the natural sugar of the meat into a browned outer layer, a nice inviting color that it would not have when cooked in the broth of a soup. When searing, turn the meat on all sides, even propping pieces up on the edge of the pan if needed.

$1/2$ **pound stew beef**
4 cups water
4 beef bouillon cubes
1 cup chopped onion
1 cup carrot slices
$1/2$ **teaspoon salt**
$1/8$ **teaspoon black pepper**
$1/4$ **teaspoon celery seed**
$1/2$ **teaspoon dried oregano**
2 cups uncooked extra wide egg noodles

Remove all fat from beef and cut into bite-size pieces. Place in a small skillet over high heat and sear all sides of the meat. Add beef to water in a 3-quart saucepan over medium high heat. Stir in bouillon, onion, carrots, salt, pepper, celery seed, and oregano. Bring to a boil. Reduce heat to low and cook, with lid slightly vented, for 10 minutes. Add noodles to the soup. Continue to cook on low with lid slightly vented for 10 minutes more. Stir and serve.

Serves 4

Calories per serving 294
Fat per serving 6g

Bowling Night Stew

Chopping an ingredient means to cut small irregular-size pieces. You accomplish this by using a cutting board and very sharp knife. One hand holds the knife tip while the other moves the blade through the food, making random cuts.

$1/2$ pound ground chuck
4 cups water
1 (8-ounce) can tomato paste
$1/2$ cup chopped onion
$1/2$ cup chopped celery
1 cup cubed potato
$1/2$ cup carrot slices
$1/2$ large green bell pepper, cut in strips
$1/2$ teaspoon salt
$1/8$ teaspoon ground cayenne pepper
1 bay leaf (do not crumble)

Cook meat thoroughly in a 3-quart saucepan over medium heat, stirring frequently to break up large pieces of meat. Drain any fat. Pour water into saucepan. Spoon in tomato paste and stir until smooth. Add onion, celery, potato, carrot, and bell pepper to stew. Stir in salt, cayenne pepper, and bay leaf. Bring to a boil over medium-high heat. Reduce heat to low. Cover, with lid slightly vented, and cook 30 minutes. Remove bay leaf before serving.

Serves 4

Calories per serving 186
Fat per serving 3g

Poultry Soups

Bay Chicken with Leeks

The long, tender white stems of leeks are protected while growing by pulling the soil up around the plant to shield it from harsh sunlight in a process known as blanching. As a result of this, dirt and sand tend to get deep between the broad, flat green leaves, so rinsing well before using is necessary.

2 boneless, skinless chicken breasts
8 cups water
2 large leeks, white and light green stems
1/2 cup diced carrot
1/2 cup quick-cook or pearl barley
1/2 teaspoon salt
1/4 teaspoon black pepper
1/8 teaspoon ground cloves
2 whole bay leaves (do not crumble)

Rinse chicken; combine with water in a 5-quart pot over high heat and bring to a boil. Reduce heat to medium. Skim foam from the top with a metal spoon. Cover, with the lid slightly vented, and cook chicken 20 minutes, or until fully cooked. Thoroughly clean the leeks, running water between the leaves. Discard the tough green feathered leaves found at the bottom of the leeks. Slice leeks into ¼-inch rounds; set aside. After the chicken is cooked, remove from water, trim any fat, then cube chicken and return to broth. Increase to high heat. Add the carrot, barley, salt, pepper, cloves, and bay leaves to the soup. Stir in the leeks. Bring to a boil. Reduce heat to medium low, cover with lid slightly vented, and cook 20 minutes. Remove bay leaves before serving.

Serves 6

Calories per serving 177
Fat per serving 2g

Chicken with Wild Rice

Wild rice is an aquatic grain with a distinctive nutty flavor. This natural product is often referred to as the "caviar of grains." While most of the wild rice we eat today is cultivated using machinery, there are still many growers who hand-gather wild rice. Due to the density of wild rice, it must be cooked longer than true rice to become soft.

1 boneless, skinless chicken breast
4 cups water
1 extra large vegetable bouillon cube (or enough
granules to make 2 cups of broth)
1/2 cup chopped onion
1/4 teaspoon dried basil
1 (4-ounce) box wild rice
1 (10-ounce) package frozen peas

Rinse chicken; combine with water in a 3-quart saucepan over high heat. Add bouillon and bring to a boil. Reduce heat to low. Skim off foam with a metal spoon. Cover, with lid slightly vented, and cook 20 minutes, or until chicken is fully cooked. Remove from the pan, leaving the broth in the pot over low heat. Cut away any fat from chicken and discard. Chop chicken into bite-size pieces and return to the broth. Add onion, basil, and wild rice to the soup. Cover with lid and continue to cook over low heat 45 minutes. Add the peas. Cover with lid and cook 10 minutes more. Stir and serve.

Serves 4

Calories per serving 238
Fat per serving 2g

Chicken Gumbo

Okra is a member of the mallow family, which also houses cotton, hibiscus, and hollyhock, and is a 3- to 10-inch green tapering seed pod with ribs down its length. Releasing a sticky juice when cut, okra has the unique ability to act as a thickening agent in soups.

1 boneless, skinless chicken breast
4 cups water
1/2 cup diced celery
1/2 cup chopped onion
1/4 teaspoon salt
Dash of black pepper
Dash of ground thyme
1/8 teaspoon dried basil
1/8 teaspoon ground cayenne pepper
1 (28-ounce) can diced tomatoes, with juice
1 cup frozen cut okra

Rinse chicken; combine with water in a 3-quart saucepan over high heat. Bring to a boil, then reduce heat to low. Skim off foam with a metal spoon. Cover, with lid slightly vented, and cook 20 minutes, or until chicken is fully cooked.

Remove chicken from broth. Measure out 2 cups broth, discarding the remainder. Pour the reserved broth back into the pan over medium heat. Remove any fat from the chicken, cube, and place back into the broth. Add celery, onion, salt, pepper, thyme, basil, cayenne pepper, and tomatoes with juice to broth. Bring to a low boil, stirring occasionally. Reduce heat to low and add okra. Cover with lid and cook 15 minutes. Remove from heat. Stir and serve.

Serves 4

Calories per serving 123
Fat per serving 1g

Turkey Sage Soup

Soup is the perfect solution to post-holiday turkey. Plan ahead and chop the turkey into bite-size pieces and freeze in 2-cup increments. Chicken and turkey provide similar taste and can be swapped in this or other recipes.

1 tablespoon butter or margarine
$1/2$ cup diced onion
8 cups water
2 chicken bouillon cubes
$1/8$ teaspoon salt
$1/4$ teaspoon ground sage
2 cups chopped cooked turkey
$1/2$ cup quick-cook or pearl barley
1 cup frozen broccoli florets

Melt butter or margarine in a 3-quart saucepan over medium heat. Add onion and sauté until tender. Add water, bouillon, salt, sage, turkey, and barley to the water. Bring to a boil. Reduce heat to low, cover with lid slightly vented, and cook 40 minutes. Add broccoli to the soup. Cover with lid and cook 5 minutes more. Remove from heat. Stir and serve.

Serves 6

Calories per serving 173
Fat per serving 4g

Humpty Dumpling Stew

Dumplings can be made with a complex list of ingredients and fillers or can be as simple as mixing flour and water. This recipe uses traditional drop dumplings.

4 cups water
1 boneless, skinless chicken breast
1/2 cup chopped onion
1 small clove garlic, pressed
1 teaspoon salt, divided
Dash of black pepper
1 cup grated carrots
2/3 cup frozen peas
1 1/4 cups flour
2 1/2 teaspoons baking powder
1/2 teaspoon dried basil
2 tablespoons vegetable oil
2/3 cup milk

Combine water and chicken in a 3-quart stockpot over high heat. Add onion, garlic, 1/2 teaspoon salt, and pepper; bring to a boil. Reduce heat to low. Skim foam with a metal spoon. Cover and cook 20 minutes, or until chicken is cooked. Remove chicken, chop into small chunks, and return to broth. Add carrots and peas.

In a small bowl, stir together the flour, baking powder, remaining salt, and basil. Mix well. Add the oil and milk, and stir until smooth.

Bring soup to a low boil over high heat (reduce heat early if boil is too aggressive). Scoop out balls of dough with two teaspoons and drop into the stew. Reduce heat to low, cover tightly with lid, and cook 10 minutes. Do not lift lid while steaming dumplings.

Serves 4

Calories per serving 330
Fat per serving 10g

Home-Style Chicken Noodle

Walking in from a cold, snowy day to a steamy kitchen where a pot of homemade chicken noodle soup bubbles on the stove and fills the air with anticipation can make a fond memory.

2 boneless, skinless chicken breasts
8 cups water
$1/2$ cup chopped onion
1 cup chopped celery pieces
1 cup carrot slices
$1/2$ teaspoon salt
$1/8$ teaspoon black pepper
$1/4$ teaspoon dried basil
2 cups broken (1-inch) spaghetti noodles

Combine chicken and water in a 5-quart saucepan over high heat. Bring to a boil, then reduce heat to medium. Cover, with lid slightly vented, and cook 20 minutes, or until chicken is fully cooked. Skim foam from the top with a metal spoon. Remove the chicken from broth when cooked, shred into bite-size strips, and return to broth.

Add onion, celery, carrots, salt, pepper, and basil to the broth. Add spaghetti to the soup. Bring to a gentle boil; reduce heat to low. Cover, with lid slightly vented, and cook 10 minutes more.

Serves 6

Calories per serving 252
Fat per serving 2g

Chicken Alfredo Soup

One of the most practical and affordable kitchen gadgets is the garlic press. It guarantees that crushing a firm clove of garlic will be a simple task.

1 boneless, skinless chicken breast
9 cups water, divided
3 chicken bouillon cubes
1 clove garlic, pressed
Dash of black pepper
¹/₈ teaspoon nutmeg
1 cup milk
1 tablespoon flour
¹/₂ cup grated Parmesan cheese
1 cup broken fettuccine noodles (1-inch pieces)
1 teaspoon dried parsley

Rinse chicken; combine with 6 cups water in a 3-quart saucepan over high heat. Bring to a boil. Reduce heat to low. Skim off foam with a metal spoon. Cover, with lid slightly vented, and cook 20 minutes, or until chicken is fully cooked. Remove chicken from pan and cube. Discard cooking water, rinse pan, and pour 3 cups fresh water into the pan over medium-high heat. Add cooked chicken, bouillon, garlic, pepper, and nutmeg. Pour milk into a tall glass, add flour, and stir rapidly with a fork until smooth. Pour milk into soup and bring to a light boil. Add cheese slowly while continuously stirring. Drop heat to low and stir in noodles. Cover, with lid slightly vented, stirring every 2–3 minutes to keep noodles from sticking, and cook for 10 minutes. Garnish with dried parsley.

Serves 4

Calories per serving 309
Fat per serving 13g

Bok Choy Chicken

A member of the cabbage family, bok choy has long white stalks that resemble celery without the stringiness. Topped by dark green curly leaves, bok choy has a light sweet flavor and a crisp texture.

1 boneless, skinless chicken breast
4 cups water
2 cups chopped bok choy pieces
¹/₄ cup diced green onions
1 cup fine egg noodles
1 tablespoon soy sauce
¹/₄ teaspoon salt
Dash of black pepper
Dash of ground ginger

Combine chicken and water in a 3-quart saucepan over high heat. Bring to a boil; then reduce heat to medium. Skim foam from top with a metal spoon. Cover, with lid slightly vented, and cook 20 minutes, or until chicken is fully cooked. Remove chicken, cube, and return to broth. Add bok choy, green onions, and noodles. Stir in soy sauce, salt, pepper, and ginger. Press vegetables down into the broth with a spoon. Reduce heat to low. Cover, with lid slightly vented, and cook 10 minutes more. Be careful not to overcook. You want vegetables to maintain a firm texture. Remove from heat and serve.

Serves 4

Calories per serving 140
Fat per serving 2g

Tortilla Chicken Soup

Put the tortilla chips and cheese into colorful self-serve side dishes to keep them from getting too mushy in the soup. To make sure the soup is still hot enough to melt the cheese, ladle it into bowls just before you are ready to begin the meal. If you would like to spice the soup up a bit, use canned tomatoes with chiles instead.

1 boneless, skinless chicken breast
10 cups water, divided
4 chicken bouillon cubes
$1/4$ cup chopped onion
1 small clove garlic
$1/4$ teaspoon salt
Dash of black pepper
$1/4$ teaspoon cumin
1 (15-ounce) can black beans, drained
1 ($14 1/2$-ounce) can diced tomatoes, drained
2 cups corn tortilla chip pieces
$1/2$ cup grated mild cheddar cheese

Combine chicken and 6 cups water in a 3-quart saucepan over high heat; bring to a boil. Reduce heat to medium. Cover, with lid slightly vented, and cook 20 minutes, or until chicken is fully cooked.

Remove chicken from pan and cube. Discard cooking water, rinse pan, and pour 4 cups fresh water into the pan over medium-high heat. Add cooked chicken, bouillon, onion, garlic, salt, pepper, and cumin. Cook 5 minutes, allowing flavors to mingle. Add black beans and tomatoes. Bring to a low boil, then reduce heat to medium. Cover, with lid slightly

vented, and cook 10 minutes. Ladle soup into serving dishes. Evenly distribute tortilla chip pieces on top of the soup, and then sprinkle with the cheddar cheese.

Serves 4

Calories per serving 582
Fat per serving 11g

Sesame Chicken with Stir-Fry Vegetables

There are many varieties of stir-fry vegetable mixes available. The colorful combination used for this recipe includes broccoli, carrots, onions, red peppers, water chestnuts, mushrooms, and celery. You can substitute other arrangements of vegetables in this recipe, keeping note of the taste, texture, and color to provide the most pleasing presentation.

1 boneless, skinless chicken breast
8 cups water, divided
4 chicken bouillon cubes
$1/8$ teaspoon ground ginger
$1/4$ teaspoon celery seed
2 tablespoons light soy sauce
$1/4$ teaspoon sesame seed oil
1 (1-pound) package frozen stir-fry vegetables
$1/2$ cup quick-cook rice

Combine chicken and 4 cups water in a 3-quart saucepan over high heat. Bring to a boil, then reduce heat to medium. Cover, with lid slightly vented, and cook 20 minutes, or until chicken is fully cooked. Remove chicken from pan and discard cooking water. Rinse pan. Chop chicken into bite-size pieces. Combine 4 cups fresh water and chicken in pan over medium-high heat. Add bouillon, ginger, celery seed, soy sauce, sesame seed oil, and vegetables. Bring to a boil, then stir rice into boiling water. Remove immediately from heat. Cover with lid and let stand 5 minutes. Stir and serve.

Serves 4

Calories per serving 239
Fat per serving 2g

Pork Soups

Split Pea with Smoked Ham

Split peas, which come in green or yellow, are left on the vine to dry naturally as whole peas. During the sorting process they are bombarded against a baffle, causing them to split in two, which speeds the cooking process.

1 (16-ounce) package split peas
8 cups water
$1/2$-pound piece boneless smoked ham
2 cups diced carrots
1 cup chopped onion
1 teaspoon salt
$1/8$ teaspoon black pepper
$1/4$ teaspoon dried tarragon leaves
1 whole bay leaf (do not crumble)

Rinse and sort split peas. Combine peas and water in a 5-quart pot over medium-high heat. Remove rind and fat from ham. Chop ham into cubes and add to peas. Stir in carrots, onion, salt, pepper, tarragon, and bay leaf. Bring to a boil, then reduce heat to low. Cover, with lid slightly vented, and cook $2\frac{1}{2}$ hours, stirring occasionally. Add an additional $\frac{1}{2}$ cup water while cooking if needed. Remove bay leaf before serving.

Serves 6

Calories per serving 360
Fat per serving 4g

Smoked Ham and Potato

Salt is an essential element in the diet of humans, animals, and even some plants. It has the distinguished mantle of being one of the most effective and widely used of all food preservatives.

2 1/2 cups thinly sliced potatoes
1/2 cup chopped onion
2 cups water
1/2 cup grated carrot
1/2-pound piece boneless smoked ham, cubed
1/2 cup milk
1/2 teaspoon salt
Dash of black pepper
1/4 teaspoon dried marjoram

Add potatoes and onion to water in a 3-quart saucepan over medium-high heat. Bring to a boil, then reduce heat to low. Cover, with lid slightly vented, and cook 10 minutes, then return heat to medium-high. Add carrot and ham to soup. Use the back of spoon to break up large pieces of potato. Stir in milk, salt, pepper, and marjoram. Bring to a boil. Reduce heat to low, cover with lid slightly vented, and cook 30 minutes, stirring occasionally.

Serves 4

Calories per serving 209
Fat per serving 6g

Smoky Broccoli

The name broccoli originates from the Italian "brocco," which means an arm or branch. There are two types of broccoli. The first grows as a dense curd similar to cauliflower and is called "heading broccoli." The second type is more commonly known and is used for this soup. It is "sprouting" or "Italian broccoli," which features a branching cluster of green flower buds sitting on a thick stalk.

2 chicken bouillon cubes
1 (10-ounce) package frozen chopped broccoli
3 cups water
$1/2$ cup milk
3 tablespoons flour
$1/4$ teaspoon salt
$1/8$ teaspoon black pepper
$1/4$ teaspoon dried basil
8 strips smoked bacon, cooked and crumbled

Add bouillon and frozen broccoli to water in a 3-quart saucepan over medium-high heat. Pour milk into a tall glass, add the flour, and stir rapidly with a fork until smooth. Add the milk mixture to soup. Stir salt, pepper, and basil into soup. Bring to a low boil, stirring occasionally to break up frozen broccoli. Reduce heat to low. Cover, with lid slightly vented, and cook 10 minutes, stirring occasionally. Remove from heat. Ladle into serving dishes and sprinkle bacon crumbles over each serving.

Serves 4

Calories per serving 361
Fat per serving 24g

Irish Cabbage Soup

When cooking with cabbage, don't be alarmed if it looks like too much for the pan. Push the cabbage pieces down into the broth with a spoon. It will cook down to about half the volume of the raw cabbage.

$^1/_2$-pound piece boneless ham, cubed
$^1/_2$ cup diced onion
$^1/_8$ teaspoon salt
$^1/_8$ teaspoon black pepper
1 extra large vegetable bouillon cube (or enough
   granules to make 2 cups broth)
4 heavily packed cups coarsely chopped green cabbage
$^1/_2$ cup grated carrot
1 (8-ounce) can tomato sauce
6 cups water
Dill weed, fresh or dried, for garnish

Add ham, onion, salt, pepper, bouillon, cabbage, carrot, and tomato sauce to water in a 3-quart saucepan over medium-high heat. Press vegetables down into broth with a spoon. Bring to a boil, then reduce heat to low. Cover, with lid slightly vented, and cook 25 minutes, stirring occasionally. Add an additional ½ cup water if needed. Ladle into serving dishes. Garnish with dill weed.

Serves 6

Calories per serving 97
Fat per serving 3g

Wonton Soup

It is best to have a few extra wonton wrappers available as you become familiar with the folding process. A few may also break in the middle as you determine the proper amount of filling. If in doubt about the folding procedure, most wonton wrapper packages have illustrated directions.

9 1/2 cups water, divided
1 tablespoon minced green onion
1/4 pound unseasoned ground pork
1 egg
2 tablespoons soy sauce, divided
1/8 teaspoon ground ginger
36–40 wonton wrappers
6 chicken bouillon cubes
1/4 cup chopped green onion, white and green part

Pour 8 cups water into a 3-quart saucepan over medium-high heat.

In a small mixing bowl, combine minced green onion, pork, egg, 1 tablespoon soy sauce, and ginger. Mix until ingredients are evenly distributed. Lay out wonton wrappers. (You will need 36 for this soup.) Bring a small bowl of water close by your work area. Place 1/2 teaspoon meat mixture in the middle of each wrapper. Wet edges of the wrapper, fold wrapper over to make a triangle and press edges together. Wet edges again, bring the two outside corners together and press down to seal edges. Lay finished wontons on a tray until you have them all completed. Place wontons into the boiling water one at a time. Use a spatula to run under the wontons to make sure they don't stick to the pan. Return water to a boil. Let wontons cook 5 minutes—they will float to the top when finished. Remove wontons with

a slotted spoon and lay on a clean plate until needed.
Discard cooking water. Pour 1½ cups fresh water
into saucepan over medium-high heat. Add bouillon,
remaining soy sauce, and chopped green onion.
Bring to a boil. Add finished wontons and cook
5 minutes. Remove from heat. Ladle into serving
bowls, giving each serving 6 wontons.

Serves 6

Calories per serving 292
Fat per serving 5g

Pork Stew

Cubing an ingredient in a recipe usually indicates a medium-size cut, ranging from a half inch to an inch in size. This method of cutting ingredients will give your recipe a more uniform appearance.

^{1}/$_2$ **pound boneless pork chops**
2 beef bouillon cubes
^{1}/$_2$ **cup chopped onion**
1 clove garlic, minced
^{1}/$_4$ **teaspoon salt**
^{1}/$_8$ **teaspoon black pepper**
^{1}/$_2$ **teaspoon dried oregano**
1 cup water
1 (16-ounce) bag frozen stir-fry vegetables

Fully cook pork chops in a small skillet, browning lightly on the outside. Remove fat from pork, cube meat, and set aside. Add cooked pork, bouillon, onion, garlic, salt, pepper, and oregano to water in a 3-quart saucepan over medium-high heat. Bring to a boil. Add vegetables. Vegetables will not be completely covered with broth but will cook down. Reduce heat to low. Cover, with lid slightly vented, and cook 5 minutes, stirring occasionally. Remove immediately from heat. (Don't overcook vegetables.) Stir and serve.

Serves 4

Calories per serving 192
Fat per serving 4g

Hoppin' John with Smoked Ham

Hoppin' John is a traditional Southern soup made with meaty ham hocks or spicy sausage. The Northern version, which isn't as taste-intense, features pork ribs or ham.

1 cup dried black-eyed peas
8 cups water, divided
$1/2$ pound smoked ham, cubed
4 chicken bouillon cubes
$1/2$ cup chopped onion
1 clove garlic, thinly sliced
$1/4$ teaspoon salt
$1/8$ teaspoon black pepper
$1/4$ teaspoon ground cayenne pepper
$1/2$ cup quick-cook rice

Sort and rinse black-eyed peas. Bring peas and 4 cups water to a boil in a 3-quart saucepan over high heat. Let boil 1 minute, then remove from heat. Cover tightly and let stand 1 hour. Drain water from peas. Add 4 cups fresh water to peas over medium-high heat. Stir in ham, bouillon, onion, garlic, salt, pepper, and cayenne pepper. Bring to a boil, then reduce heat to low. Cook, with lid slightly vented, for 90 minutes. Add rice to the soup. Cook 10 minutes more. Stir and serve.

Serves 4

Calories per serving 391
Fat per serving 6g

Italian Sausage Soup

Zucchini is a perfect vegetable to buy from the farmers market during mid-summer when it is in season and plentiful. Peel and grate the zucchini. Freeze in 2-cup increments. It is a satisfying filler for soups and stews when old man winter comes calling.

1/2 pound Italian sausage
1 (14 1/2-ounce) can diced tomatoes, with juice
1/2 cup orzo pasta
1 cup chopped onion
1 clove garlic, thinly sliced
1 cup shredded zucchini
2 cups water
1/4 teaspoon salt
1/8 teaspoon black pepper
1/2 teaspoon dried oregano
1 green bell pepper, chopped

Cook sausage thoroughly, breaking into bite-size pieces as you stir. Drain fat from meat. Add cooked sausage, tomatoes with juice, pasta, onion, garlic, and zucchini to water in a 3-quart saucepan over medium-high heat. Stir in salt, pepper, and oregano. Bring to a boil. Reduce heat to low. Cover, with lid slightly vented, and cook 10 minutes. Add the bell pepper. Cover and cook 5 minutes more. Stir and serve.

Serves 4

Calories per serving 204
Fat per serving 8

Spicy Sweet Potato and Pork Soup

Sweet potatoes are a vegetable with a hard texture and can be tough to cut. In order to obtain more uniform cubes, use a sharp knife and cut sweet potato into 1/2-inch rounds. Then cube each round.

1/2 **pound boneless pork chops**
1 **(14 1/2-ounce) can petite diced tomatoes**
   with green chiles
1/2 **pound sweet potato, peeled and cubed**
1/2 **cup chopped onion**
2 **chicken bouillon cubes**
1/2 **teaspoon ground cumin**
2 **cups water**
1 **cup frozen corn**
1/4 **cup minced green bell pepper**

Fully cook pork, remove fat, and cube meat. Add cooked pork, tomatoes, sweet potatoes, onion, bouillon, and cumin to water. Bring to a boil. Reduce heat to low. Cover, with lid slightly vented, and cook 10 minutes more. Ladle into serving dishes and sprinkle each serving with bell pepper.

Serves 4

Calories per serving 212
Fat per serving 5g

Rosemary Pork with Rice

Cauliflower florets are an easy substitute for the broccoli in this recipe. When cutting vegetable florets down to an edible size, slice just above the stem where it starts to branch out. This will allow the smaller stems to separate. Save your stems; put them in a baggie and freeze. They will be perfect for the next pot of vegetable soup.

$^1/_2$ **pound boneless pork chops**
4 chicken bouillon cubes
$^1/_2$ **teaspoon crushed rosemary leaves**
$^1/_8$ **teaspoon salt**
4 cups water
2 cups frozen broccoli florets, partially thawed
$^1/_2$ **cup quick-cook rice**

Fully cook pork, remove any fat, and cube meat. Add cooked pork, bouillon, rosemary, and salt to water in a 3-quart saucepan over medium-high heat. Bring to a boil, then reduce heat to low. Cover, with lid slightly vented, and cook 10 minutes. Cut any large broccoli florets in half. Add broccoli and rice to soup. Cover and cook over low heat 5 minutes more. Stir and serve.

Serves 4

Calories per serving 218
Fat per serving 4g

Seafood Soups

Fisherman's Chowder

The wispy dill is a versatile plant with a strong personality. The seeds are used in pickling spice, and the feathery leaves known as dill weed are used fresh or dried. This garden favorite is comfortable seasoning a recipe or serving as the garnish.

**1/2 pound cod fillets (or any mild white fish),
    fresh or frozen**
1/2 tablespoon butter or margarine
1/2 cup chopped onion
2 1/2 cups water
1 1/2 cups diced potato
1/4 teaspoon salt
1/8 teaspoon black pepper
1/2 teaspoon prepared horseradish
1/2 cup milk
1 1/2 tablespoons flour
1 medium firm tomato
Dill weed for garnish, fresh or dried

Thaw fish if frozen. Remove any skin or bones from fish and cut into 1/2-inch pieces; set aside. Melt butter or margarine in a 3-quart saucepan over medium heat. Add onion and sauté until tender. Pour water over onions. Add fish, potato, salt, pepper, and horseradish to soup. Bring to a boil, then reduce heat to low. Cover with lid and simmer 20 minutes. (Potatoes should be falling apart.) While the chowder is cooking; pour milk into a tall glass. Add flour to the milk and stir rapidly with a fork until smooth;

set aside. Peel skin from tomato and cut into ½-inch pieces; set aside. After 20 minutes, stir milk mixture once or twice and add to chowder. Bring to a quick boil over high heat. Remove from heat immediately. Add tomato pieces; cover with lid and let stand 5 minutes. Ladle into serving dishes and garnish with dill weed.

Serves 4

Calories per serving 139
Fat per serving 3g

Inland Seafood Stew

Minced Alaskan Pollock, a mild-flavored white fish, is the primary ingredient in imitation crabmeat. More economical than real crab, the imitation "sticks" or "legs" are more readily available in non-coastal areas.

4 chicken bouillon cubes
1 (15-ounce) can diced tomatoes, with juice
4 cups water
1/2 cup chopped celery pieces
1/2 cup chopped onion
1/4 teaspoon lemon pepper
1/4 teaspoon ground mace
1/2 pound imitation crabmeat, stick or "leg" style
2/3 cup frozen peas

Add bouillon and tomatoes with juice to water in a 3-quart saucepan over medium-high heat. Stir in celery, onion, lemon pepper, and mace. Bring to a boil, then reduce heat to low. Cover, with lid slightly vented, and cook 15 minutes. Rinse imitation crabmeat sticks thoroughly. Slice each lengthwise and cut into 1-inch pieces. Add imitation crabmeat and peas to stew. Cover, with lid slightly vented, and cook 10 minutes more.

Serves 4

Calories per serving 88
Fat per serving <1g

Manhattan Clam Chowder

New York has been long famous for not only great Broadway productions but for big bowls of steaming clam chowder featuring tomatoes as the leading lady.

1 (6 ½-ounce) can chopped clams in clam juice
1 extra large vegetable bouillon cube (or enough
granules to make 2 cups broth)
1 cup chopped celery
1 (14 ½-ounce) can diced tomatoes, with juice
1 (8-ounce) can tomato sauce
1 cup water
Dash of black pepper
¼ teaspoon dried thyme
4 slices bacon, cooked crisp and crumbled

Drain clams, reserving juice. Add reserved clam juice, bouillon, celery, tomatoes with juice, and tomato sauce to water in a 3-quart saucepan over medium-high heat. Stir in pepper and thyme. Bring to a low boil, then reduce heat to low. Cover, with lid slightly vented, and cook 10 minutes. Add clams to chowder. Cover tightly with lid and cook 3 minutes. Ladle into serving dishes. Garnish each serving with crumbled bacon.

Serves 4

Calories per serving 255
Fat per serving 12g

New England Clam Chowder

When cooking bacon as an ingredient in a recipe, take care to remove it from the pan after cooking. Lay the bacon on paper towels to drain any excess fat.

1 (6$\frac{1}{2}$-ounce) can minced clams in clam juice
3 cups cubed potatoes
1 cup chopped celery
1 cup chopped onion
2 cups water
1 clove garlic, pressed
$\frac{1}{2}$ teaspoon salt
$\frac{1}{8}$ teaspoon black pepper
$\frac{1}{8}$ teaspoon dried thyme
2 whole bay leaves (do not crumble)
$\frac{1}{4}$ cup milk
2 tablespoons flour
4 slices bacon, cooked crisp and broken into quarters

Drain clams, reserving juice. Add clam juice, potatoes, celery, and onion to water in a 3-quart saucepan over medium-high heat. Stir in garlic, salt, pepper, thyme, and bay leaves. Bring to a boil. Reduce heat to low. Cover, with lid slightly vented, and cook 5 minutes. Pour milk into a glass. Add flour to milk and quickly stir with a fork until smooth. Add the milk mixture to chowder and cook 5 minutes more. Add clams, cover tightly with lid, and cook 3 minutes. Remove bay leaves from chowder. Ladle into serving dishes. Garnish each serving with bacon pieces.

Serves 4

Calories per serving 347
Fat per serving 13g

Salmon Balls with Rice

The combination of ingredients used to make the salmon balls are a mix used for years by my mom to make salmon patties. An old recipe with a new twist.

1 (6-ounce) can boneless, skinless pink salmon, drained
1 egg
$1/2$ teaspoon salt
$1/8$ teaspoon black pepper
$1/2$ cup self-rising flour
1 tablespoon vegetable oil
4 cups water
4 chicken bouillon cubes
$1/2$ teaspoon dried oregano
1 cup quick-cook whole grain brown rice
1 green bell pepper, chopped

Use a small bowl and mix together the salmon, egg, salt, pepper, and flour. Stir until all ingredients are well blended. Shape salmon into 24 small balls. Lay on a plate until needed. Heat vegetable oil in a skillet over medium-high heat. Add the salmon balls to hot skillet, then reduce heat to medium. Brown salmon balls on all sides. (Be careful not to turn until browned on the bottom or they may come apart.) Remove from pan; set aside. Pour water into a 3-quart saucepan over medium-high heat. Add bouillon, oregano, and rice. Bring to a boil, then reduce heat to low. Cover, with lid slightly vented, and cook 10 minutes. Add bell pepper. Cover, with lid slightly vented, and cook 5 minutes more. Remove from heat. Ladle soup into serving dishes. Add 6 salmon balls to each serving.

Serves 4

Calories per serving 332
Fat per serving 8g

Quick Shrimp and Vegetable Soup

When you want your vegetables to maintain a firm texture, watch your cooking time carefully. Overcooking by a mere 5 minutes can turn some vegetables mushy. Be sure to remove the pan from the heat source to stop the cooking process.

2 chicken bouillon cubes
$1/4$ teaspoon salt
Dash of black pepper
$1/8$ teaspoon ground cayenne pepper
2 cups cooked baby shrimp
2 cups water
1 (16-ounce) bag frozen deluxe stir-fry vegetables

Add bouillon, salt, pepper, cayenne pepper, and shrimp to water in a 3-quart saucepan over medium-high heat. Bring to a boil. Reduce heat to low. Cover, with lid slightly vented, and cook 5 minutes. Add frozen vegetables. Cover tightly with lid and cook 5 minutes more. Remove from heat. The vegetables will retain a firm texture. Stir and serve.

Serves 4

Calories per serving 185
Fat per serving 1g

Jambalaya

Jambalaya is for those who prefer their food on the spicy side. You may want to use only half the amount of crushed red pepper. Taste the broth after cooking 10 minutes and then decide if you need to spice it up.

2 chicken bouillon cubes
1 cup chopped onion
1 clove garlic, minced
1 green bell pepper, chopped
1$^1/_4$ cups small cooked shrimp
2 cups water
1 (14$^1/_2$-ounce) can diced tomatoes, with juice
1 (8-ounce) can tomato sauce
$^1/_4$ teaspoon salt
$^1/_8$ teaspoon black pepper
$^1/_2$ teaspoon crushed red pepper
1 cup quick-cook whole grain brown rice

Add bouillon, onion, garlic, bell pepper, and shrimp to water in a 3-quart saucepan over medium-high heat. Stir in tomatoes with juice, tomato sauce, salt, pepper, and red pepper. Bring to a boil, then reduce heat to low. Cover, with lid slightly vented, and cook 10 minutes. Add the rice. Continue to cook over low heat 5 minutes more with lid vented. Remove from heat, cover tightly with lid, and let stand for 5 minutes before serving.

Serves 6

Calories per serving 200
Fat per serving 1g

Easy Crab Bisque

Simple and economical garnishes for soups are at your fingertips. Reserve a small amount of a colorful vegetable in the recipe. Mince and sprinkle on top for a perfect finish.

2 chicken bouillon cubes
1 cup sliced potato
1 cup chopped onion
2 cups water
1 cup chopped celery
1 (14 $^1/_2$-ounce) can diced tomatoes, drained
1 (6-ounce) can fancy white crabmeat (do not drain)
$^1/_8$ teaspoon salt
$^1/_8$ teaspoon cumin
$^1/_8$ teaspoon ground cayenne pepper

Add bouillon, potato, and onion to water in a 3-quart saucepan over medium-high heat. Set aside 8–10 pieces of chopped celery for garnish. Add the remaining celery, tomatoes, and crabmeat to water. Stir in salt, cumin, and cayenne pepper. Bring to a boil. Reduce heat to medium. Cover, with lid slightly vented, and cook 10 minutes. Pour into a blender and purée. Ladle the bisque into colorful serving dishes. Mince the reserved celery and garnish each serving.

Serves 4

Calories per serving 105
Fat per serving <1g

Liberty Bay Gumbo

"Flexible" and "no fuss" are perfect descriptive words for gumbo. If you are short on time, go ahead and preassemble ingredients in the pan up to twenty-four hours prior to using. Gumbo also freezes well, which makes taking care of leftovers a snap.

2 chicken bouillon cubes
1/2 cup chopped onion
1 clove garlic, pressed
2 cups water
1 (14 1/2-ounce) can diced tomatoes, with juice
Dash of black pepper
1/8 teaspoon ground cayenne pepper
2 whole bay leaves (do not crumble)
2 cups frozen cooked baby shrimp
2 cups frozen okra pieces

Add bouillon, onion, and garlic to water in a 3-quart saucepan. Stir in tomatoes with juice, pepper, cayenne pepper, and bay leaves. Bring to a boil. Reduce heat to medium. Cover, with lid slightly vented, and cook 5 minutes. Add shrimp and okra. Continue to cook with lid vented for 25 minutes. Remove bay leaves. Stir and serve.

Serves 4

Calories per serving 155
Fat per serving 1g

Crab Dumplings with Broccoli

An easy way to work your dumpling batter is with this method: scoop out 1/2 teaspoon dumpling mix with one spoon while using a second spoon to nudge the dumpling into the broth. In this recipe, small pieces of the crab dumpling will break off during cooking and thicken the soup.

1/2 cup flour
1 teaspoon baking powder
1/4 teaspoon salt
1/4 teaspoon dried marjoram
1 teaspoon vegetable oil
1/4 cup milk
1 (6-ounce) can fancy white crabmeat, drained
4 cups water
4 chicken bouillon cubes
2 cups frozen broccoli florets, lightly thawed

In a small bowl, combine the flour, baking powder, salt, and marjoram; mix well. Stir in oil, milk, and crabmeat. If you have "lump" crabmeat, break it down with a fork before adding. Use 2 spoons and shape 32 mini dumplings. Place on a plate until needed. Pour water into a 3-quart saucepan; add bouillon. Bring to a boil. Add dumplings to boiling liquid. Reduce heat to low. Cover tightly with lid and cook over low for 10 minutes. Cut large broccoli florets in half. Drop broccoli into soup without stirring. Don't disturb the dumplings. Replace lid tightly and continue cooking 5 minutes more. Ladle into serving dishes.

Serves 4

Calories per serving 146
Fat per serving 2g

Vegetable Soups

Cabbage De'Lite

Eaten raw or cooked, the versatility of cabbage is one of its strongest assets. Although there are many varieties available, this recipe was made with green cabbage, which has a round head and light green compact leaves. Cabbage can be stored in the refrigerator for up to two weeks before using.

1 cup minced carrot
1 cup minced celery
$1/2$ cup minced onion
4 beef bouillon cubes
$1/4$ teaspoon dried marjoram
$1/8$ teaspoon black pepper
4 cups water
4 heavily packed cups coarsely chopped cabbage
1 tablespoon dried dill weed

Add carrot, celery, onion, bouillon, marjoram, and pepper to water in a 3-quart saucepan over medium-high heat; bring to a boil. Reduce heat to low. Add cabbage to broth, pressing down into the broth with a spoon. Cover, with lid slightly vented, and cook 5 minutes. The cabbage will retain a firm texture when the soup is finished. Ladle into serving dishes and sprinkle dill weed on each serving.

Serves 6

Calories per serving 35
Fat per serving <1g

Late Summer Garden Soup

Squash, a relative of the pumpkin, comes in two varieties. This recipe uses the quick growing summer squash, which has thin skin and is eaten before the skin and rind begin to harden. Winter squash, such as the acorn squash, have hard rinds and seeds and can be stored for longer periods of time.

2 chicken bouillon cubes
¹/₂ cup chopped onion
¹/₈ teaspoon salt
¹/₈ teaspoon black pepper
¹/₂ teaspoon dried oregano
¹/₂ teaspoon olive oil
4 cups water
1 cup chopped tomato
1¹/₂ cups diced cucumber
1 cup diced yellow squash
1 small green bell pepper, cut into thin strips
1 cup grated carrot

Add bouillon, onion, salt, pepper, oregano, and olive oil to water in a 3-quart saucepan over medium-high heat. Bring to a boil. Reduce heat to low and add all of the vegetables. Cover tightly with a lid and cook 5 minutes. Remove from heat and ladle into serving dishes. The vegetables will retain a firm texture.

Serves 6

Calories per serving 36
Fat per serving <1g

Quick & Easy Borscht

Although variations of borscht are as numerous as the countries in which it is served, all share the beetroot as a primary ingredient. Served warm or chilled, this beautiful burgundy-colored soup fully realizes its heritage when accompanied by a basket of thick brown bread.

1 (15-ounce) can sliced beets, packed in water
4 beef bouillon cubes
1/2 cup minced onion
2 cups packed coarsely chopped cabbage
4 cups water
1 tablespoon lemon juice
1/2 teaspoon dill weed, fresh or dried
4 tablespoons sour cream

Drain liquid from beets, cut each slice into shoestring pieces, and set aside. Add bouillon, beets, onion, and cabbage to water in a 3-quart saucepan over medium-high heat. Add lemon juice and dill weed to soup. Bring to a light boil, stirring occasionally. Reduce heat to low. Cover, with lid slightly vented, and cook 5 minutes; remove from heat. Serve warm or chilled. Before serving, top with a dollop of sour cream.

Serves 4

Calories per serving 171
Fat per serving 12g

Potato String Soup

The aromatic cumin seed (pronounced "come in")
is best known for its warm earthy flavor. This hand-
harvested seed is a key player in Southwestern recipes
as well as a principal in curry and chili powders.

3 cups heavily packed grated potatoes
6 chicken bouillon cubes
$1/2$ teaspoon ground cumin
1 teaspoon salt
6 cups water
$1/3$ cup diced green onions

　　Place potatoes in a bowl of cold water so they won't
turn brown; set aside. Add bouillon, cumin, and
salt to water in a 3-quart saucepan over high heat.
Bring broth to a boil. Drain potatoes and add to the
broth, immediately reducing heat to low. Cover with
lid and cook 5 minutes, stirring frequently. Remove
from heat. (Do not overcook.) Potatoes should retain
firmness. Ladle soup into serving dishes and garnish
with green onion.

Serves 6

Calories per serving 59
Fat per serving <1g

Southern Vegetable Julienne

The turnip is one of the rare vegetables where both the sharp-flavored leaves and mild-tasting roots of the plant are desirable. The slightly fuzzy turnip greens are traditionally cooked in a broth seasoned with a piece of salt pork while the firm white turnip root is eaten raw or used in soups.

4 chicken bouillon cubes
$1/4$ teaspoon salt
$1/4$ teaspoon ground allspice
4 cups water
$1/2$ cup chopped onion
$3/4$ cup julienned carrot
$1/2$ cup julienned turnip
$1/2$ cup julienned beet

Add bouillon, salt, and allspice to water in a 3-quart saucepan over medium-high heat. Stir in vegetables. Bring to a light boil. Reduce heat to low. Cover, with lid slightly vented, and cook 7–10 minutes. (Do not overcook.) Vegetables should retain a firm texture. Remove from heat and serve.

Serves 4

Calories per serving 34
Fat per serving <1g

Fresh Green Bean Soup

When choosing fresh green beans for this soup, you want to look for firm beans without blemishes. Wash the beans well. Cut the hard ends from the bean, pulling the end down the seam of the bean, which will remove any strings. Snap the beans, or cut straight across or on a diagonal if you want a more uniform appearance. You want pieces about 1-inch long. You can substitute two (14.5-ounce) cans of cut green beans (drained), if needed.

1 cup diced potato
1 cup minced carrots
¹/₂ cup chopped onion
3 chicken bouillon cubes
2 whole bay leaves (do not crumble)
Dash of black pepper
3 cups water
1 pound fresh green bean pieces (about 4 cups)

   Add potato, carrots, onion, bouillon, bay leaves, and pepper to the water in a 3-quart saucepan over medium-high heat. Bring to a boil. Add green beans, then reduce heat to low. Cover, with lid slightly vented, and cook 10 minutes. Remove bay leaves before serving.

Serves 6

Calories per serving 51
Fat per serving <1g

French Onion Soup

Using a yellow storage onion will provide a tangy, sweet flavor perfect for this recipe. Be sure to sauté the onions over medium heat as using high heat will impart a bitter taste.

2 tablespoons butter or margarine, plus more
2 cups chopped onions
$1/2$ cup minced celery
4 cups water
4 beef bouillon cubes
4 thick slices French bread
1 (8-ounce) package grated mozzarella cheese
1 tablespoon chives for garnish

In a deep skillet, melt butter or margarine over medium heat. Add onions and celery to skillet. Sauté until tender and starting to brown. Pour water into skillet and add bouillon. Bring soup to a light boil. Stir and remove from heat. Turn oven broiler to low. Place four individual ovenproof serving dishes on a baking sheet. Ladle soup into serving dishes. Spread additional butter or margarine on both sides of French bread. Place the bread in the same skillet used to make the soup. Lightly brown the bread over medium heat. Lay a slice of browned bread on top of the soup in each serving dish. Sprinkle cheese generously over each piece of toast. Top each serving with chives. Place the baking sheet in the oven. Leave soup under the broiler until cheese is melted and lightly browned. Serve immediately.

Serves 4

Calories per serving 286
Fat per serving 6g

Greek Lemon Soup

The herb savory comes in two seasons as well as dual strengths. The annual summer savory, with its peppery thyme flavor, accents soups, beans, and vegetables, and is sold commercially. Winter savory, which is a perennial, has robust pine accents and is used primarily with hearty game meats.

6 chicken bouillon cubes
$1/8$ teaspoon salt
$1/8$ teaspoon ground savory
6 cups water
$1/2$ cup quick-cook rice
2 eggs
3 tablespoons lemon juice
1 tablespoon chives for garnish

Add bouillon, salt, and savory to water in a 3-quart saucepan over medium-high heat. Bring to a boil, then reduce heat to low. Add rice to the broth; cover, and cook 5 minutes.

In a small bowl, beat eggs with a fork until well blended. Mix lemon juice into eggs. Holding the bowl over the saucepan, slowly pour in the eggs, stirring constantly. Leave the soup over low heat for 5 minutes, stirring occasionally. Ladle into serving dishes and garnish with chives.

Serves 6

Calories per serving 80
Fat per serving <1g

Marjoram Mushroom

To expedite the cooking process for this recipe, prepare and refrigerate a few ingredients a day ahead of time. Prepare the minced celery and sliced mushrooms, then cover with foil or plastic wrap. Make sure the chopped onions are in an airtight container. Cut the potatoes no more than two hours before needed, immerse in a bowl of cold water (with a hint of lemon if you have it), and drain prior to use.

2 chicken bouillon cubes
1/3 cup minced celery
1/2 cup chopped onion
2 cups water
2 cups cubed potatoes
1/4 teaspoon salt
1/8 teaspoon black pepper
1/2 teaspoon dried sweet marjoram
1 (12-ounce) package sliced mushrooms
2 cups milk

Add bouillon, celery, and onion to water in a 3-quart saucepan over medium-high heat. Add potatoes and stir in salt, pepper, and marjoram. Bring to a boil. Reduce heat to low; cover with lid slightly vented and cook 10 minutes. Return heat to medium-high. Add mushrooms and milk to soup. Bring to a quick low boil, reducing heat immediately to low. Cover, with lid slightly vented, and cook 10 minutes more.

Serves 6

Calories per serving 106
Fat per serving 3g

Mushroom Barley Soup

Each extra large vegetable bouillon cube makes 2 cups of prepared broth. If you do not find the extra large cubes, use smaller cubes or granules according to the package specifications to make the same amount of broth as the extra large cubes.

1 tablespoon butter or margarine
$^1/_2$ cup chopped green onions, white and green stems
1 cup chopped celery
$^1/_2$ pound fresh mushrooms, thinly sliced
6 cups water
2 extra large vegetable bouillon cubes (or enough
  granules to make 4 cups broth)
$^1/_4$ teaspoon dried oregano
$^1/_2$ cup quick-cook or pearl barley

In a 5-quart pot, melt butter or margarine over medium heat. Add the onion, celery, and mushrooms. Sauté until tender, stirring frequently. Pour water over vegetables. Add bouillon, oregano, and barley. Bring to a light boil. Reduce heat to low, cover with lid, and cook 15 minutes.

Serves 6

Calories per serving 90
Fat per serving 2g

Italian Cauliflower Soup

Parmigiano-Reggiano is the Italian name for what we know as Parmesan cheese. The light-colored Parmesan can have a taste range from mild and smooth to dry and crumbly, depending on the number of months the cheese is allowed to mature.

2 chicken bouillon cubes
2 cups cauliflower florets
1/4 cup chopped onion
4 cups water
1 small clove garlic, pressed
1/2 tablespoon olive oil
1/2 teaspoon salt
Dash of black pepper
1/4 teaspoon dried oregano
1 (6-ounce) can tomato paste
1 cup broken angel hair pasta
2 tablespoons grated Parmesan cheese for garnish

Add bouillon, cauliflower, and onion to the water in a 3-quart saucepan over medium-high heat. Add garlic and stir in olive oil, salt, pepper, and oregano. Add the tomato paste and stir until well blended with no lumps. Bring soup to a low boil, then reduce heat to low. Add noodles. Cover, with lid slightly vented, and cook 20 minutes, stirring occasionally. Remove from heat. Ladle into serving dishes and garnish with Parmesan cheese.

Serves 4

Calories per serving 188
Fat per serving 3g

Vegetable Barley

Growing wild in the mountain ranges of Greece, oregano is called "joy of the mountains," reflecting the Greek "oros," which means mountain, and "ganos," which means joy. The pungent oregano shows up in many of the same dishes as its milder cousin marjoram.

$1/2$ **cup chopped onion**
$1/2$ **cup chopped celery**
1 cup carrot slices
2 extra large vegetable bouillon cubes
$1/2$ **cup quick-cook or pearl barley**
$1/2$ **teaspoon dried oregano**
8 cups water
2 cups broccoli florets

Add onion, celery, carrot, bouillon, barley, and oregano to water in a 5-quart pot over medium-high heat. Bring to a boil, then drop heat to low. Cover with lid and cook 15 minutes. Add broccoli florets to soup. Cover with lid and cook 5 minutes more.

Serves 6

Calories per serving 88
Fat per serving <1g

Titillating Tortellini

Tortellini belongs to the family of "ripiena" or filled pastas. Ravioli and manicotti are also in this category. Meat, along with herbs and various cheeses, used as a group or independently, are the best-known filling ingredients for tortellini. You will find tortellini in the refrigerator section of your grocery store.

6 chicken bouillon cubes
4.5 ounces cheese tortellini (35 pieces)
1/2 cup diced red bell pepper
1/2 teaspoon dried basil
6 cups water
2 cups packed torn spinach

Add bouillon, tortellini, bell pepper, and basil to water in a 3-quart saucepan over high heat. Bring to a boil, then reduce heat to medium. Cover with lid and cook 10 minutes. Add spinach to broth. Cook, uncovered, 3 minutes more. Remove from heat and serve.

Serves 6

Calories per serving 49
Fat per serving 2g

Spinach Soup

Hinting at mild oregano with a splash of balsam, the pale grey-green leaves and minute clusters of flowers belonging to sweet marjoram are a complement to many other herbs, including bay and garlic.

1 envelope dry onion soup mix
1 cup diced potato
1/4 teaspoon salt
1/8 teaspoon dried marjoram
4 cups water
1 (10-ounce) package frozen chopped spinach
1 cup grated mild cheddar cheese

Add soup mix, potato, salt, and marjoram to water in a 3-quart saucepan over medium-high heat. Bring to a light boil, then reduce heat to low, cover with lid, and cook 5 minutes. Drop in spinach, stirring frequently to break up. Cover with lid and cook 20 minutes over low heat. Ladle into serving dishes and garnish with cheese.

Serves 4

Calories per serving 208
Fat per serving 10g

Stir-Fry Noodle Soup

Blending well with lemon, garlic, and basil, thyme offers a dainty green taste with hints of clove and is most at home in French, Creole, and Cajun cuisine. Stir-fry noodles used in this recipe are found in the international section of the grocery store. They come woven tightly together.

2 chicken bouillon cubes
$^1/_2$ cup chopped onion
$^2/_3$ cup frozen peas
$^1/_2$ cup grated carrot
$^1/_4$ teaspoon salt
$^1/_8$ teaspoon black pepper
$^1/_2$ teaspoon dried thyme
6 cups water
1 (6-ounce) package dried stir-fry noodles

Add bouillon, onion, peas, carrot, salt, pepper, and thyme to water in a 3-quart or larger pan over medium-high heat. Bring to a boil, then reduce heat to medium, cover, and cook 10 minutes. Break the stir-fry noodles into bite-size pieces and add to soup. Cover with lid and cook 2–3 minutes more. Remove from heat, keep covered, and allow to stand 15 minutes before serving.

Serves 6

Calories per serving 117
Fat per serving <1g

Nacho Cheese with Potatoes

As a convenience, frozen hash browns were used in this soup. If you have fresh potatoes, substitute 3 cups grated potatoes for the 4 cups frozen. Fresh grated potatoes are generally larger than frozen hash browns. Increase cooking time to 5 minutes if using fresh grated potatoes.

2 chicken bouillon cubes
$1/2$ cup chopped onion
2 cups water
$1/4$ teaspoon salt
$1/2$ teaspoon dried crushed red pepper
1 (8-ounce) package processed cheese, cubed
4 cups frozen hash brown potatoes
1 tablespoon dried chives

Add bouillon and onion to water in a 3-quart saucepan over medium-high heat. Stir in salt and red pepper. Bring to a boil, then reduce heat to low. Add cheese to broth. Stir continuously until cheese is melted. Add hash brown potatoes to the soup. Cover completely and cook over low heat for 2 minutes. (Do not overcook.) Remove from heat. Stir and ladle into serving dishes. Garnish each serving with chives.

Serves 4

Calories per serving 392
Fat per serving 26g

Mama's Easy Potato Soup

Not too spicy, and long heralded as comfort food, this easy potato soup is perfect for the days you are feeling a little under the weather and need . . . just a little something.

5 cups thickly sliced potatoes
1 cup chopped onion
2 tablespoons butter
$1/2$ teaspoon salt
$1/4$ teaspoon black pepper
1 tablespoon dried chives
4 cups water

Add potatoes, onion, butter, salt, pepper, and chives to water in a 3-quart saucepan over medium-high heat. Bring to a boil, then reduce heat to medium. Cover, with lid slightly vented, and cook 10 minutes. Remove from heat. Stir and serve.

Serves 6

Calories per serving 143
Fat per serving 4g

Gazpacho

Vegetables fresh from your garden or the local farmers market provide the taste that propels gazpacho into top position as the perfect summer soup. Gazpacho stores well, so it is worth the time to make a double batch to have on hand for sweltering August days.

2 beef bouillon cubes
1 (15-ounce) can tomato sauce
1/2 teaspoon olive oil
1 tablespoon Worcestershire sauce
1/2 cup minced onion
1/8 teaspoon salt
1/8 teaspoon ground cayenne pepper
2 cups water
1 green bell pepper, sliced
2 cups chopped tomatoes
1 cup diced cucumbers

Add bouillon, tomato sauce, olive oil, Worcestershire sauce, onion, salt, and cayenne pepper to water in a 3-quart saucepan over medium-high heat. Bring to a boil, then reduce heat to low. Cover, with lid slightly vented, and cook 5 minutes. Remove from heat. Add bell pepper, tomatoes, and cucumber to soup; stir well and let cool. Cover tightly with lid and refrigerate at least 3 hours before serving. Serve chilled.

Serves 6

Calories per serving 43
Fat per serving <1g

Matzo Ball Soup with Chives

The word "matzo" means a plain flour-and-water dough that has been rolled flat and baked until it is the consistency of a cracker. It is then ground into matzo meal, which has the look and feel of cornmeal.

2 eggs
2 tablespoons vegetable oil
1 (2 1/2-ounce) packet matzo ball mix
2 teaspoons dried chives, divided
6 chicken bouillon cubes
1 cup grated carrot
6 cups water

In a small bowl, combine eggs, oil, matzo ball mix, and 1 teaspoon chives. Stir until all ingredients are evenly distributed. Cover and refrigerate 15 minutes.

Add bouillon, carrot, and remaining chives to water in a 3-quart saucepan over medium-high heat. Bring to a rolling boil. Wet hands and form matzo balls, using 1 tablespoon dough for each ball (about 12). Drop balls into the boiling broth. Reduce heat to low; cover tightly with lid and cook 20 minutes. Do not lift lid while steaming matzo balls. Ladle into serving dishes, giving each serving 2 balls.

Serves 6

Calories per serving 117
Fat per serving 6g

Tomato Basil Soup

Basil, with its mild pepper flavor enhanced by a hint of mint and clove, is available in fourteen varieties with a leaf color ranging from pale green to deep purple. It is easy to grow indoors or in the garden. Basil also dries well with a home dehydrator. Remove the leaves from the stems, dry leaves, and store in a canning jar.

4 chicken bouillon cubes
2 cups chopped celery
$1/2$ cup minced onion
$1/4$ teaspoon dried basil
1 (8-ounce) can tomato sauce
4 cups water
2 cups chopped tomatoes

   Add bouillon, celery, onion, basil, and tomato sauce to water in a 3-quart saucepan over medium heat. Bring soup to a light boil, reduce heat to low. Cover, with lid slightly vented, and cook 5 minutes. Add tomatoes to soup. Cover with lid and cook 5 minutes more. (Do not overcook.) Vegetables will retain a firm texture. Remove from heat and serve.

Serves 6

Calories per serving 28
Fat per serving <1g

Fruit Soups

Blueberry Jo

The sweet flavor and creamy texture of this soup makes it especially attractive to children. Dixie cup servings are a delicious and healthy treat for birthday parties or snack time. This unique soup can be prepared ahead of time and stored in an airtight container in the freezer. Partially thaw and stir before serving.

**1 (1-pound) package dry pack frozen blueberries
  (do not thaw)
1 cup water
1 (6-ounce) container blueberry yogurt
2 tablespoons honey
1/8 teaspoon ground cinnamon
1/2 cup light cream**

Place frozen blueberries into a blender, reserving 12 for garnish. Add water, yogurt, honey, and cinnamon to blueberries. Purée until smooth. Pour cream into soup and blend until evenly distributed. Pour into chilled serving dishes and garnish with the reserved blueberries.

Serves 4

*Calories per serving 175
Fat per serving 7g*

Strawberry Cream Soup

The fragrant mint, with its distinguishing square stem, encompasses a broad assortment of flavors, from chocolate to pineapple. However, the most commonly used mint in cooking is spearmint, with its mild unobtrusive ability to blend without overpowering.

1 (1-pound) package frozen strawberries, partially thawed
1/3 cup pulp-free orange juice concentrate, thawed
1 cup water
1 tablespoon lime juice
1/4 cup honey
1 cup light cream
1 teaspoon dried mint leaves

Place partially thawed strawberries into a blender, reserving 4 to 6 whole berries for garnish. Add orange juice concentrate, water, lime juice, honey, cream, and mint leaves. Purée until smooth. Ladle soup into serving dishes. Thinly slice the reserved berries and position the small ends together in the middle of soup adding 3 per serving.

Serves 6

Calories per serving 154
Fat per serving 7g

Cool Harvest Apple

The Golden Delicious apple is perfect for this recipe. It has a firm texture that will hold up to being grated as well as presenting a consistent taste. Several other good choices would be Jonagold, Braeburn, or Fuji apples.

3 large firm, cooking apples
1 (12-ounce) can frozen apple juice concentrate,
without sugar
1 juice can water
2 teaspoons lemon juice
$^1/_4$ teaspoon ground cinnamon
$^1/_2$ cup light cream

Peel and grate apples (about 3 cups). Place grated apples into a blender. Add frozen apple juice concentrate and water to the apples. Add lemon juice, cinnamon, and cream. Blend until cream is evenly distributed (approximately 10 seconds). Leave lid on blender and place in the freezer for 1 ½ hours. Stir and serve icy cold. If desired, garnish each serving with a dash of cinnamon.

Serves 6

Calories per serving 110
Fat per serving 4g

Peaches 'n' Cream Soup

Unlike most herbs and spices, cinnamon doesn't come from a leaf. It is the inner bark that is peeled away from the small tender evergreen cinnamon tree. As the bark dries, it will curl into sticks that are called quills. These quills are used ground or whole.

1 (1-pound) package frozen peaches, partially thawed
1 cup cold water
$1/8$ teaspoon ground cloves
$1/8$ teaspoon ground cinnamon
$1/4$ cup honey
1 (6-ounce) container peach yogurt
1 cup light cream

Place peaches into a blender, reserving $1/4$ cup for garnish. Add water, cloves, cinnamon, and honey. Purée until smooth. Add the yogurt and cream. Blend until ingredients are evenly distributed. Place blender, with lid on, in the freezer for 45 minutes. Remove from the freezer, stir, and spoon into chilled serving dishes. Mince the reserved peaches, and sprinkle evenly onto each serving.

Serves 6

Calories per serving 210
Fat per serving 8g

Tropical Chill

You want to use a ripe melon for this recipe. A ripe cantaloupe should be a little soft when you squeeze it and will have an intense melon smell. If you buy your ingredients for this soup a few days early, you can buy a harder melon. Leave it out on the counter to ripen at room temperature.

1 large ripe cantaloupe (approximately 4 cups purée)
1 (12-ounce) can frozen pineapple juice concentrate, thawed
2 tablespoons lemon juice
1/8 teaspoon ground cinnamon

Peel and halve cantaloupe, removing all seeds. Slice the fruit into strips lengthwise, and then quarter each strip. Reserve 1 cup cantaloupe chunks for garnish.

Place the cantaloupe into a blender and purée. You may have to do this in batches. Add the pineapple concentrate, lemon juice, and cinnamon. Run on the blend cycle until all ingredients are evenly distributed. Place blender in the freezer for 2 hours. Remove soup, stir, and ladle into chilled serving dishes. Dice reserved cantaloupe and sprinkle equally onto each serving.

Serves 6

Calories per serving 67
Fat per serving <1g

Orange Mist

Fruit soups can be frozen for one or two hours and have a soup consistency or you can leave them in the freezer for a longer period of time and serve as a sorbet.

1 (12-ounce) can pulp-free orange juice concentrate, partially thawed
1 cup water
1 cup heavy cream
$^1/_2$ teaspoon vanilla
$^1/_8$ teaspoon nutmeg
1 firm fresh orange

Pour orange juice concentrate into a blender. Add water, cream, vanilla, and nutmeg. Blend until smooth. Place blender in the freezer for 1 hour. Remove from freezer, stir and ladle into serving dishes. Wash fresh orange and remove ends. Use a sharp knife to make thin slices. Float an orange ring in each serving.

Serves 4

Calories per serving 267
Fat per serving 22g

Mango Tango

Choosing a ripe mango depends upon three elements: a bright-colored skin, a tropical scent by the stem end, and a soft feel. However, fingers should not leave an indention where they touched.

2 large ripe mangos, cubed
1 (12-ounce) can limeade frozen concentrate,
**   partially thawed**
1/2 cup water
1/2 cup heavy cream
1/8 teaspoon allspice
2 tablespoons honey

Set aside 1/4 cup cubed mango for garnish. Place remaining mango into a blender. Add remaining ingredients. Blend until smooth. Place blender, with lid on, in the freezer for 2 hours. Remove from freezer and stir. Ladle into serving dishes. Mince the reserved mango and sprinkle over each serving.

Serves 4

Calories per serving 233
Fat per serving 11g

Mixed Berry Soup

The berry mix I used for this recipe was a delightful combination of strawberries, blueberries, red raspberries, and blackberries. Create your own mix: When you serve fresh berries with a meal, save a small handful in an airtight freezer container. Keep adding until you have 2 cups of various berries.

1 (12-ounce) can fruit punch frozen concentrate, partially thawed
1 cup water
1 cup heavy cream
1 teaspoon vanilla
¹/₄ teaspoon cinnamon
1 (15-ounce) package frozen mixed berries, partially thawed

Pour fruit punch concentrate into a blender. Add water, cream, vanilla, and cinnamon. Purée until smooth. Reserve a half cup of the darker berries; set aside. Add the remaining berries to the blender and purée until smooth. Ladle soup into chilled serving dishes. Garnish each serving with the reserved berries.

Serves 6

Calories per serving 240
Fat per serving 15g

Cherries Jubilee

Partially thawed juice is loose around the edges and should allow the concentrate to easily release from the can while the middle is still frozen. This will take about 10 minutes.

1 (11.5-ounce) can frozen cranberry juice concentrate, partially thawed
1 (21-ounce) can cherry pie filling or topping
¹/₂ cup heavy cream
¹/₈ teaspoon cinnamon

Pour cranberry concentrate into a blender. Spoon the cherries out of the can. Mash each cherry with a fork to check for pits. Reserve 4 cherries for garnish. Add the remaining cherries, cream, and cinnamon to the blender. Purée until smooth. Place blender in the freezer for 1 hour. Stir and ladle into serving dishes. Mince the reserved cherries and sprinkle over each serving.

Serves 4

Calories per serving 336
Fat per serving 11g

Maui Sunset

With this soup, place a kiwi circle in the middle of the soup. Slice three strawberries, while they are still frozen, into 4 thin pieces, lengthwise. Put the wide ends of the strawberries against the kiwi circle and you have a flower.

**1 (12-ounce) can frozen limeade concentrate,
    partially thawed**
2 peeled and sliced kiwi
**1 (16-ounce) package frozen dry-pack strawberries,
    partially thawed**
¹/₄ cup water
1 teaspoon vanilla
¹/₈ teaspoon cinnamon

Pour the limeade into a blender. Reserve 4 kiwi slices and 3 or 4 frozen strawberries for garnish. Place the remaining kiwi and strawberries in the blender. Add water, vanilla, and cinnamon. Purée until smooth. Ladle into chilled serving dishes. Garnish each serving with kiwi and strawberry slices.

Serves 4

Calories per serving 75
Fat per serving <1g

Sources

Smith, Andrew F. *Souper Tomatoes: The Story of America's Favorite Food.* New Brunswick: Rutgers University Press, 2000. Information on history of soups. Used with author's permission.

American Dry Bean Board
www.americanbean.org

American Egg Board
www.aeb.org

California Fresh
Apricot Council
www.califapricot.com

Christmas Point Wild
Rice Company
www.christmaspoint.com

The Epicentre—
Encyclopedia of Spices
www.theepicentre.com
Barry Mortin, author

Food Reference
www.FoodReference.com
Chef James T. Ehler

Italian Trade Commission
www.italianmade.com

Leafy Greens Council
www.leafy-greens.org

Leek Growers Assoc.
of Great Britain
www.british-leeks.co.uk/

Mann Packing Company Inc.
www.broccoli.com

McCormick & Company Inc.
www.mccormick.com

National Barley Foods Council
www.barleyfoods.org

National Garden Bureau
www.ngb.org

Rhonda Parkinson, author,
The Chinese Cuisine Site
www.chinesefood.about.com

Salt Institute
www.saltinstitute.org

USA Dry Pea & Lentil Council
www.pea-lentil.com

Vegetarians in Paradise,
Internet magazine
www.vegparadise.com
Zel and Reuben Allen

Special Thanks To:
www.deliciousitaly.com, "Bite sized portions of information for the independent traveler to Italy who knows how to eat and travel well."

Index

Metric Conversion Chart

Volume Measurements		Weight Measurements		Temperature Conversion	
U.S.	Metric	U.S.	Metric	Fahrenheit	Celsius
1 teaspoon	5 ml	½ ounce	15 g	250	120
1 tablespoon	15 ml	1 ounce	30 g	300	150
¼ cup	60 ml	3 ounces	90 g	325	160
⅓ cup	75 ml	4 ounces	115 g	350	180
½ cup	125 ml	8 ounces	225 g	375	190
⅔ cup	150 ml	12 ounces	350 g	400	200
¾ cup	175 ml	1 pound	450 g	425	220
1 cup	250 ml	2¼ pounds	1 kg	450	230

Coming from generations of Southern "pinch of this" cooks, **Gayle Pierce** learned at a young age how to combine flavors and textures from ingredients she had on hand. She has been gathering and testing soup recipes on family and friends for more than twenty years. She resides in Liberty, Indiana.